Kind Words about Stretch Marks I

"Relatable in the deepest recesses of the heart. Abbie captures the questions of life without wrapping the answers in a neat little package. She powerfully allows the reader to wonder alongside her, giving the reader an unusual gift: the freedom to think, process and ponder. Stretch Marks I Wasn't Expecting is a journey you will not want to miss."
Jennifer Walker RN BSN, author and co-founder of Momsoncall.com

"*Stretch Marks I Wasn't Expecting* sucked me in with its beautiful and prayerful reflections on the joys and challenges of motherhood. Abbie does a masterful job of bringing the reality of 'noisy graces' to the fore and demonstrating that we too are being formed even as we seek to disciple and form our children. Read and hand out to the mothers you know - and dads too!"
Marlena Graves, author, *A Beautiful Disaster: Finding Hope in the Midst of Brokenness*

"Through heartfelt internal dialogue and honest reflection, Abbie Smith brings her reader on a journey depicting the laboring life and unpolished struggles of early motherhood. She asks questions we're afraid to ask and unveils thoughts others are embarrassed to admit regarding concerns of infertility, bonding with a newborn, post-partum depression, and issues of body image. Smith weaves her personal experience with her intimate pursuit of Christ, acknowledging the effects that motherhood has on both marriage and spirituality. I highly recommend this book to anyone craving personal growth and self-reflection. Smith's beautiful form of writing and incorporation of scripture is both thoughtful and enjoyable for its reader."
Juli Windsor, PA-C and public speaker

"Read it with a sigh of relief. Stretch Marks I Wasn't Expecting is permission to be human and broken, vulnerable and unfinished - to shed the unmet expectations of ourselves and the perceived expectations of others. I wish I could read these words to my younger self. This well-articulated reprieve is a must read for young women and mothers of young children. Abbie's memoir will make you laugh and cry and say, 'Thank GOD I'm not the only one.' Enjoy painting yourself into one of Abbie's stories or descriptions as she gently dispels the feminine fantasies of first comes love, then comes baby and replaces them with the intimate reality of Jesus."
Salina Beasley, wife & mother of four, singer-songwriter

"Filled with laughter, tears, searing honesty and gorgeous writing, this is one of the best reads of the year. Quite simply, this is a stunning book. Smith writes about motherhood in such a way that whether you have had children or not you can relate to having Stretch Marks you don't expect. Let the gentle waves of this prose wash over you and water your soul."
Amy Young, author of *Looming Transitions* and *Love, Amy*

"Abbie's beautiful gift of writing paints a vivid picture that many of us live but struggle to assign words. Sharing her life on pages with us provides a safe space to relate, feel understood and be challenged to grow in the grace and truth of Jesus, our only true hope."
Elizabeth Dixon, wife, mom, speaker, and manager of hospitality strategy, Chick-fil-A

"The writing alone is a portal into a beautiful soul. But the insights, candor and honesty are an invitation to see oneself through the lens of grace and truth. Every woman should read this! Every man who has ever loved a woman should be required to read this beautiful roadmap into a woman's soul!"
Stephen W. Smith, President and Spiritual Director of Potter's Inn and author of the best selling, *The Lazarus Life*

STRETCH MARKS
I WASN'T EXPECTING

STRETCH MARKS
I WASN'T EXPECTING

a memoir on early marriage and motherhood

Abbie Smith

God cannot love you more than he does in this moment. —Abbie

Kalos Press—an imprint of Doulos Resources
2017

Stretch Marks I Wasn't Expecting
Published by:
Kalos Press—an imprint of Doulos Resources, 195 Mack Edwards Drive, Oakland,
TN 38060; PHONE: (901) 201-4612 WEBSITES: www.kalospress.org; www.
doulosresources.org.

Published 2017
Printed in the United States of America by Ingram/Lightning Source
Colophon:
Cover design by Caroline Fausel; interior design by Caroline Fausel
Copyediting by Anna Barber; proofreading help provided by Jessica Snell.
Typefaces include Garamond Pro (body text set in 11pt.); Roboto
This book is printed using 50lb. 444 ppi "crème" archival paper that is produced
according to Sustainable Forestry Initiative® (SFI®) Certified Sourcing.
Smith, Abbie, 1981–
Stretch Marks I Wasn't Expecting
ISBNs: 978-1-937063-36-8 (print); 978-1-937063-35-1 (digital)
                                                              2017955474
13   14   15   16   17   18   19   20   10   9   8   7   6   5   4   3   2

Micah, my best friend and soulmate, what a profound grace to share this story with you. Elliana, Eden, & Aaliya, these are but the fringes of how your glory-filled lives have stretched and shaped mine. What a privilege to be your Mommy.

TABLE OF CONTENTS

PREFACE

I heard the snap as the wafer broke during communion last Sunday. Normally I'm many rows back and distracted at this point in the service—by someone's new haircut, or getting up to use the bathroom—but for a few reasons I've been sitting up front lately. And this week, I literally heard the crack as the element was torn in two. It's an act that's been performed thousands of times before, in thousands of places on the planet, yet the sound was immaculately fresh this day.

And he took bread, and when he had given thanks, he broke it and gave it to them, saying, "This is my body, which is given for you. Do this in remembrance of me."

—*Luke 22:19 (NASB)*

A few mornings removed, I'm still pondering the sounds of Communion and the severity of Jesus' giving. His body broken, horribly, for the whole world. Mine is being broken by a process more ordinary. Gazing down at chipped toenail polish, amber hardwoods beneath beckon to my attention. Grains in the heart pine swerve expressively, some dull, some dramatic, as if to form a narrative—etchings of proof that life has been lived on this ground. The longer I stare, the more stories I begin to see, the more scuffs and indentations documenting a weight of humanity: curiosity and grief, fatigue and wisdom, justice and romance, despair and growth. The lines in the wood seem to mimic marks on my skin—stretch marks—etchings of proof that life has been lived on this ground; this ordinary, *holy* ground.

Blissful though matrimony is in many senses, it's interrupted my relationship with God—someone else is in our space. Having babies has interrupted it all the more—*someone else was in my body*—then integrated into what feels like every crevice of my daytime and nighttime being. At times I've felt trapped, launched into a deep end of sorts and unsure where the sidewall is, let alone how to swim there. Speckled across the same canvas as some of life's most blissful moments are unexpected hues of disillusion and resentment, boredom and a lost sense of purpose. Learning to find beauty in this mix has become a daily plea; learning to find meaning in it has become a desperate one.

Is there meaning in these early years of marriage and motherhood? I've wondered this often in recent years. While chopping an onion, or staring at a stained pile of whites, I've wondered if maybe "Image-bearer of God" was a title haphazardly acquired back when my days were doing something important. Monotonies of wiping and bathing and wiping again don't seem to carry quite the same dignity. Am I worth loving if I've done nothing worth posting today? It sounds ludicrous, but we wake to an insane pressure to edit and filter and share images of our day until they seem worthy of liking—until we seem worthy of liking maybe. I wonder if you've wondered such things.

Is not the bread which we break a sharing in the body of Christ?

—I Corinthians 10:16b

Dearest Reader, knowing many are vying for your energies this hour, I don't take it lightly that you have opened these pages. They aren't anything fancy; my story isn't anything fancy. But I do hope you'll find it welcoming and real, with plenty of space for your own narrative to safely weave throughout. And I hope you'll find a recurrent theme of remembrance that we are loved and we are liked, and that is enough— maybe that is everything.

Regardless of the stage we're in, I believe we are, in fact, Image-bearers with extraordinary meaning. What an honor to bear life alongside you.

Love,

Abbie

1. CHOPPED

"Real isn't how you are made," said the Skin Horse. "It's a thing that happens to you. When a child loves you for a long, long time, not just to play with, but REALLY loves you, then you become Real."

"Does it hurt?" asked the Rabbit.

"Sometimes," said the Skin Horse, for he was always truthful. "When you are Real you don't mind being hurt."

"Does it happen all at once, like being wound up," he asked, "or bit by bit?"

"It doesn't happen all at once," said the Skin Horse. "You become. It takes a long time. That's why it doesn't happen often to people who break easily, or have sharp edges, or who have to be carefully kept. Generally, by the time you are Real, most of your hair has been loved off, and your eyes drop out and you get loose in the joints and very shabby. But these things don't matter at all, because once you are Real you can't be ugly, except to people who don't understand."

—The Velveteen Rabbit, Margery Williams

I've decided what screws us up most in life is the image in our head of how life is supposed to be. Tweezers searched for grays this morning to anxiously pluck from my head. Nine times out of ten, this seductive habit reflects a deeper plucking. Lately it's been about my identity, learning what it means to be whole. Particularly when I don't feel whole, but chopped, as if grabbing for something, or a part of my someone, to hold onto. Obvious identities might be,

Abbie the author

Abbie the wife

Abbie the mom

Atlanta Abbie

Friend of God, Abbie

Abbie in college

Abbie Sprünger

Abbie Smith

Overseas Abbie

Abbie in graduate school

Savannah Abbie

Depressed Abbie

Well-with-soul Abbie

Abbie the athlete

Abbie the anorexic

Abbie at this church

or season

or stage of life...

As a young teen, I remember sitting cross-legged on the beige carpet in my bedroom, sketching pregnant women with charcoal. I didn't know about sciatica, or reflux, or ferocious bouts with morning sickness, but I knew something about femininity was mesmerizing. *I knew something about the shape of expectancy was beautiful.*

Writing out this list doesn't feel beautiful or expectant though, but overwhelming. Unlike the smoothness of charcoal, it feels choppy. *I* feel choppy. And chopped. Into so many tiny pieces struggling to decipher who is *me?* So many longings in search of a sturdy *I*. My mind tries to remember. My soul tries to grasp. But no identity holds. None seems indicative of my whole, none all the way true. In an email exchange the other day, my friend Berry proposed, "What if somehow all the identities are all the way true?"

....

A handful of Augusts ago, my Camry and I made our way across Route 10, from seminary in L.A., to an uncharted life in Savannah, Georgia. Visiting a church one Sunday, a cute guy assisting a blind, black man on his arm sat by me during the opening hymn. That was January and we married in October.

In a nutshell, Micah stops at yellow lights and I go through them. He was raised by missionary parents in rural Japan; I was raised by tennis playing parents in suburbia Atlanta. He played in the graveyard behind the Buddhist Temple and went to boarding school in the Philippines; I swam the 50-fly for our country club and wore a plaid skirt to Catholic High School. Fresh to the States and Covenant College, Micah began trudging through the mud of American Christianity; off to Emory University to play tennis, I got sidelined by Jesus.

Christianity wasn't compelling to me because I was bad, per se, but more so I think because I was tired—tired of trying, and tired of hiding inner cacophonies of longing at that nineteen-year-old ledge of my story. I heard that Jesus did all the trying necessary, to the point of death, and that I was allowed to unloose my grip on holding up the planet. Life had always stayed trapped in a rule for me, being either black or white, good or bad, sin or not sin. Though behaviorally I stayed mostly on the "not sin" sides, I never felt free. Around that time someone said to me, "God cannot find you more precious than He does in this moment, Abbie." I guess I still felt like I could be found more precious. Thus began my conversion, a lifelong pilgrimage awakening to God's love.

In some sense, I'm still where I was in the beginning. Tired at some level, full with cacophonies of longing and a desire to be known anew as infinitely precious—to know God anew as infinitely precious. "Hope is one of our duties," Wendell Berry says. "A part of our obligation to our own being and to our descendants is to study our life and our condition, searching always for the authentic underpinnings of hope. And if we look, these underpinnings can still be found."[1] I believe this. I see hope in many hours of the day. But I also hear whispers of despair, seductions toward where I *should* be at this point in my life. Maybe Henri Nouwen was right in saying that "Joy is hidden in sorrow and sorrow in joy. If we try to avoid sorrow at all costs, we may never taste joy, and if we are suspicious of ecstasy, agony can never reach us either. Joy and sorrow are the parents of our spiritual growth."[2] Maybe I'm just not there yet.

---

1 Berry, Wendell. "The Art of the Commonplace". In *The Agrarian Essays of Wendell Berry*, edited by Norman Wirzba, 321-338 (Berkeley, CA: Counterpoint Press, 2003).
2 Henri J. M. Nouwen, "Bread for the Journey: A Daybook of Wisdom and Faith," in *Our Spiritual Parents*, January 2. (New York City, NY: HarperOne, 2006).

A friend poured sugar in her coffee last night as she spoke the painful words of her life not being where she'd envisioned. "I feel childish and stupid with my longings," she lamented. It seemed obvious to note that her longings resembled those of a child, and to encourage her to stay *there*, in that prerequisite-for-heaven[3] place. It seemed obvious to recall God's adoration for children, and the "years of child" in this friend—the four-year-old, the seven-year-old, the nine-year-old—and the invitation to pray from these places. It seemed obvious to remind her, "For he satisfies the longing soul, and the hungry soul he fills with good things."[4] I wish the scrutinizing gal in my mirror had such obvious observations, but instead she curses and coerces and plucks disapprovingly. Apparently it's easier to see truth making its way through another than to notice the truth in ourselves.

Our first assignment in graduate school was to offer our name, place of origin, and greatest desire and fear for the semester. In a room of about thirty adults, the most commonly voiced fear was basically, "I'm scared of another let-down; I'm scared that hard-fought efforts will end with another disappointment and further disguised self, like the rest of my life."

....

Pulling away from neurotic attempts with the tweezers, I decided to search for the words "season" and "longing" in the Bible. It didn't take long to start remembering that all seasons invite other seasons and tend soil for the next.[5] All longings invite others, and ultimate longings for Home.[6] God is not in one season, or age, or longing, but all. My soul started to

---

3 See Matthew 18:3.
4 Psalm 107:9.
5 See Acts 1:7–8.
6 See II Corinthians 5:2.

breathe, remembering maybe I am not one season, or age, or longing, but many, wrapped into many, written into many, converted during many, held by One, as God's beloved daughter, Abbie.

Maybe this stage of my conversion is less about a ledge and more about finding roots, and rootedness in living more alive as *me*. No doubt it would be easier to create an identity than to believe I'm born into one, and *being* born into one. It would seem more savvy to make up an image than to seek one I've been becoming since the beginning. But this is what I'm committing to, digging beneath a surface of ease and savviness, searching for a sturdier soil on which to stand.

Maybe the journey resembles the story of a rose. Should one attempt to pull open its petals by hand, growth is severed and the plant eventually dies. But should one find patience enough to trust a work beyond immediate place and pace of growth, involving soil and sun, water and waiting, one might eventually witness the splendor of a bloom. It's daunting to believe such a creativity has been forging its way through me since my inception; it's daunting to believe I behold a bloom. Yet something of that splendor seems worth my unseen endeavors. For something of the shape of expectancy still strikes me as alluringly beautiful.

> *...even to your old age I am he,*
>
> *and to gray hairs I will carry you.*
>
> *I have made, and I will bear;*
>
> *I will carry and will save.*
>
> *—Isaiah 46:4*

2. WOMB

Infertile

Feels

Insecure

Incapable

Inferior

Denied

Inhuman

Inept

Unable

Absent

Unfeminine

Undone

Insufficient

Rejected

Empty

Hope

Unseen

Ask

Covet

Why

Grieve

Wait

My assumption is that the story of any one of us is in some measure the story of us all.

—Frederick Buechner[7]

---

7   Frederick Buechner, *The Sacred Journey: A Memoir of Early Days* (San Francisco, CA:Harper One, 1991), 6.

I remember staring at the chipped white trim on my downtown balcony, sharing with Micah news of endometriosis and likelihoods that I may never become pregnant—not the sexiest words from a soon-to-be-wife's mouth. I grieved with Hannah about my infertility, my inability to offer the gift of offspring to the man next to me, so desperately, so fervently; the priest Eli would've thought me drunk too. Hannah vowed to God that should He give her a child, she promised to give him back.[8] *Can I promise this, Father, this sacrificial faith and surrender?* Actually I'm not even sure I have that energy in me, feeling instead an empty quiver of despair. Though I'd always dreamed of adoption, I'd also always dreamed of carrying a child.

At least one time as a young girl, I remember standing in front of the mirror and puffing my belly out. I didn't know how one becomes pregnant, but I did know Mary became pregnant *differently*—somehow divinely. And maybe I could too. Maybe I could be a new Mary, another carrier to a sacred infant. Years later, I *do* know how one becomes pregnant (and still marvel at the divine fashioning). And I do still dream of looking down at a protruded belly, not from puffing, but from bearing life to a sacred infant.

In sobering quiet, Micah held my hand, and the sun bowed into the horizon as if to remind our sorrow that it was holy ground, and new mercies would be here in the morning. Some hours later, still raw and exposed, alone in the flowered chair by the window, a strand of scribbles stood out in the margin of my Bible: "To steward well my singleness, I must believe a greater end is coming. To wait well this season, I must trust a story bigger than the one I see." It sounded lovely for my some-years-back July 28th self, but far-flung from where I was tonight.

---

8 See I Samuel 1:1-19.

My twenties told an inspiring story of being a "season of waiting," for a spouse, life direction, job, security in my own skin, place to call home, etc. (And let's be honest, the spouse piece felt like it could accomplish 99 percent of my serenity and partner with me in finding the other 1 percent). Soon after that scribble in my margin, I came down with malaria while living in Jinja, Uganda. I was on a bus heading toward Kampala to hang out for the weekend. Not a comfy bus with cup holders, but more like a boisterous stadium hallway, with loud chickens and screaming babies on a one-way dirt road (just pretend like cars or buses don't come from the other direction). And sweat; lots of sweat. Mind you, this is one of my favorite countries in the world, but when the forces of malaria hit you on a ride that lasts anywhere from two to five hours, it's not a pretty sight. Especially when that ride *only* stops at its destination, and due to lacking hospital and hotel options at that destination, your *only* option is to immediately turn right back around and ride that same bus for two to five hours back to your starting point. Oh, and malaria will kill you if you don't find treatment quickly enough.

Lord, how do I wait well now? How do I withstand hours of seeming agony when all I can envision is this parasite creeping aggressively around my body? How do I trust you? How do I survive this ride, let alone the bumpy, thirty-minute one on the rear of a bike when back in my village? And then a ten-minute walk to the clinic? How do I wait well on the diagnosis, then through the five days letting the parasite run its course?

A few years removed, I found myself in another season waiting on God. New to Savannah, without a church home or friends and still with no prospects of my 99 percent, I cried out: *God, I believe you led me here. Why, and for what purpose though? For how long? I'm tired of waiting. Do you really know the steps for this season of my life? Do you really have a precise and prevailing plan for how all this is going down?* A few months later, of course, I met Micah. He is dreamy, but hasn't cured my waiting woes. My parenthetical list remains lengthy. *When will this bout of depression lift, or frustrations with that lessen? When will he change? When will I change? And most recently, why are you ignoring my hopes for pregnancy?*

The "non-mom-voice" has been taunting me for a number of weeks. *Why don't you have babies yet? You've been married over a year. Your clock is ticking. Your womb is wasting away.* I've tried to ignore it, but that's only seemed to invite deeper and more persistent taunts. *What's wrong with you? What's wrong with your body? Everyone else is having babies and is wondering why you're not.* Feeling David-sized in my voice this morning, up against a Goliath-sized pack of lies, I'm attempting a response.

"You are wrong. Your taunts and arguments are wrong. You clearly do not know my God." Teary and uncomposed, I continued. "You don't understand that my God gives his daughters a different womb—a womb about a Kingdom. If God should ever give me a child who calls me mommy, I shall be terrifically grateful. But if He doesn't, there are multiple other means by which He has positioned my practice of motherhood. As a woman, I've been asked to dream with the broken, and disciple hope and a future into the flock behind. As a womb-bearer, I've been given space to invite the hurting into marriage with the Bearer of life, freedom, and healing. And these are but the fringes. These are but a taste of the astonishing roles for which my mothering heart has been created."

I haven't heard the non-mom-voice again today. But when I do, please remind me of these words.

For weeks now, her barren figure has waited by the French doors in our kitchen. The coral orchid who once adorned the stem lost her petals last month. This morning, however, nature sang forth a new bud.

Every season is pregnant with something, I'm starting to think. Every season beckoning something of new birth. At four, I carried joy in lightning bugs and the taste of strawberry ice cream through hot Georgia summers. At fourteen, I bore angst over awkward thighs, and acne, and wishing I were 21. At 21, I grew dreams of falling in love and traversing all corners of the world. Wonder leads me yet, a gentle, fluttering dance inside me, beckoning a story beyond what I can see.

Maybe to be pregnant is to carry—captivations of romance and joy, insecurity and longing, loneliness and hope. Maybe to be pregnant is to bear existence beyond one's self, cultivating space for maturation and fragility, tearing down and *being made new.* Maybe to be pregnant is to recognize invisible breaths in dying, and beauty in mundane living, to be penetrated by faith, *the substance of things hoped for, the evidence of things not seen.* Maybe to be pregnant is to surrender to circumstance and waiting, to belief and breath, as means of growth and mediators of birth.

There's a story in the Old Testament about a most admirable woman, and yet we're never told her name. We know her family and whereabouts and how she conducted her days, but we know not what she was called. Her story is told in Judges 11, when her dad makes a vow to God:

> *Then the Spirit of the LORD came on Jephthah. He crossed Gilead and Manasseh, passed through Mizpah of Gilead, and from there he advanced against the Ammonites. And Jephthah made a vow to the LORD: "If you give the Ammonites into my hands, whatever comes out of the door of my house to meet me when I return in triumph from the Ammonites will be*

the LORD's, and I will sacrifice it as a burnt offering." Then Jephthah went over to fight the Ammonites, and the LORD gave them into his hands. He devastated twenty towns from Aroer to the vicinity of Minnith, as far as Abel Keramim. Thus Israel subdued Ammon.

When Jephthah returned to his home in Mizpah, who should come out to meet him but his daughter, dancing to the sound of timbrels! She was an only child. Except for her he had neither son nor daughter. When he saw her, he tore his clothes and cried, "Oh no, my daughter! You have brought me down and I am devastated. I have made a vow to the LORD that I cannot break." "My father," she replied, "you have given your word to the LORD. Do to me just as you promised, now that the LORD has avenged you of your enemies, the Ammonites. But grant me this one request," she said. "Give me two months to roam the hills and weep with my friends, because I will never marry." "You may go," he said. And he let her go for two months. She and her friends went into the hills and wept because she would never marry. After the two months, she returned to her father, and he did to her as he had vowed. And she was a virgin.⁹

Jephthah's daughter died with no husband. She died without ever planning a wedding, or making love, or hearing the laughter of her child. She died with no visible legacy, and yet a legacy worth recording in the canon of Scripture. I wonder today if part of it is because she knew how to celebrate. I thought my dad hung the moon, but I can't remember running to him in jubilant song and dance beyond the age of about eight. Why? Maybe because kids celebrate better than adults do. Maybe we "mature people" get stuck in our fancy insecurities that need a glass of wine to walk freely. It also seems that Jephthah's daughter knew how to grieve. She knew God could handle her pain, and that space and time and community were vital in counseling her aching soul. She knew grief was the way to joy, to hope beyond the hopeless hour before her.

---

9 Judges 11:29-39 (New International Version).

Jephthah's daughter desired a husband, badly, and yet God had somehow awakened in her a desire for something else—something bigger and more vital. She acknowledged her desires to marry and have sex and bear children, and grieved letting them go. Not in hopes of getting them back, but in belief that grief was the road to life beyond their loss. Maybe she knew something about the grief of the Cross coming before the gain of the Resurrection.

Returning inside from pulling plush handfuls from our compost, I'm reminded this morning that life isn't always visible. But life is always the foundation of the visible. "For from him and through him and to him are all things."[10] God not only allows our laments, but he records them in his Word, someday I suppose, knowing we'll look back at them, astounded by the particular and spectacular love that planned even our darkest hours. Nature is singing forth a new bud.

Holy Spirit, I need help believing the scribbles in my margin again, that "to steward well this hour, I must believe a greater end is coming. To wait well this season, I must trust a story bigger than the one I see." I need help believing no person, or place, or outcome will satisfy my waiting today. That all my vacant and various realms of waiting amount to the appearing of the glory of our great God and Savior,[11] who for the joy set before him endured the cross, despising the shame, and is seated at the right hand of the throne of God.[12]

---

10 Romans 11:36.
11 See Titus 2:11–13.
12 See Hebrews 12:1–2.

3. ACHE

This is the blessed life—not anxious to see far in front, nor careful about the next step, not eager to choose the path, nor weighted with heavy responsibilities of the future, but quietly following behind the Shepherd, one step at a time.

The Oriental shepherd was always ahead of his sheep. He was down in front. Any attack upon them had to take him into account. Now God is down in front. He is in the tomorrows. It is tomorrow that fills men with dread. God is there already. All the tomorrows of our life have to pass Him before they can get to us.

—F.B. Meyer, Streams in the Desert

I like winter because I like scarves and s'mores and freedom to go braless to the grocery store in my hefty winter coat. I also don't like winter because cold and dark can feel like the prevailing season—a season of "always winter, but never Christmas," like Mr. Tumnus said.[13]

Absurdities from this season hit me differently each year. As a child, it involved the fat fella with the red suit, and searching for the crack of dawn with my sister Courtney on Christmas morning. As I got older, I began to wonder why *we* exchange gifts for someone else's birthday? When I started believing the Jesus part of the Christmas story, the absurdities turned more absurd, like "for us men and for our salvation, he came down from Heaven, and was incarnate by the Holy Spirit and the virgin Mary, and was made man."[14] Deity became humanity; a teenage virgin became pregnant with God. A king born into poverty, an adolescent Christ who increased in wisdom and stature,[15] learning to walk and talk, to read and tell the truth, and who in his twenties wrestled with doubt and desire.

Through and after college, I remember hating trips home for Christmas. More than weddings and Valentine's and Mother's Day. I hated being so aware of the romance—the magic of couples needing each other's warmth, strolling with lattes on snowy sidewalks as they shopped and giggled and wore cute boots. I struggled with boisterous tables of eggnog and festive china clashing with sensations of vacancy. I hated coming home to a purple bedroom with gymnastics trophies from when I was nine, then falling asleep on the basement couch to reruns of Pacey and Dawson and microwaved popcorn. I remember being seated at the kids' table on Christmas Eve when I was 19; it was worse than getting pubic hair.

---

13 C.S. Lewis, *The Lion, the Witch, and the Wardrobe* (United Kingdom: Geoffrey Bles, 1950).
14 Quoted from "The Nicene Creed," adopted in 325 by the First Council of Nicaea and today is the most widely used statement of core beliefs in Christianity.
15 See Luke 2:52.

The Jesus part of it seemed real, and really powerful somehow, even when I wasn't into Jesus, but somehow it was never enough. Never the crux of what my heart experienced each December. My singleness felt bigger, deeper, lonelier. My twenties meant my sister and every childhood friend getting married, then having babies. Visits turned into meeting their maturing families. I was angry and wanted to blame someone, especially when they'd tilt their head and change their voice and say something like, "Any special someones in your life, Abbie? Maybe this new year is when you'll meet him. What about that guy from high school prom? Or the one who joined the Peace Corps; he seemed nice?"

Coming home meant trying to get away from home, to coffee shops, running trails, boxes of cereal, Anne Lamott books—anything to be with something other than the *without* I felt at home. I craved escape, and yet knew I still craved home somehow. Being at home *with* someone, or something I couldn't give a language for. Home was what I hated. And yet somehow my deepest longing was hidden in my deepest hatred. "The ache for home lives in all of us," said Maya Angelou, "the safe place where we can go as we are and not be questioned."[16] I have the guy now and magical lights beam through pine needles in our living room. But if I listen closely enough, the homeward longing still lingers.

....

Today is cloudy. A bird just shat on me. No tree overhead, no nest, no nothin'—he had the whole universe at his disposal and chose the two millimeter crevice behind my left ear. I used to marginalize depression. I used to think it was only loonies in the looney house who experience it. Now I know I'm a looney, too.

---

16 Maya Angelou, *All God's Children Need Traveling Shoes* (New York: Vintage Books, 1991).

One can have the most marvelous husband, I've decided, and friends and Maker and job and church and health and neighborhood and weather and home and still battle depression. One can partake in the most vivacious and widespread of travels and life experiences and still fight a periodic fog against clarity and clear-minded thinking. "The demon of *acedia*— also called the noonday demon—is the one that causes the most serious trouble of all," Kathleen Norris writes. "He makes it seem that the sun barely moves, if at all... he instills in the heart of the monk a hatred for the place, a hatred for his very life itself."[17]

Neighbors invited us for a party last week. An honor in theory, and an unarguable answer to prayer. Uncomfortable in reality, posing a wider scope of prayers. We're the minority in our transitional neighborhood, locally dubbed "the hood." Stenches of weed and nicotine alongside margaritas crowded with tequila met us at the door. It was obvious we were the minority, and chances for light seemed pitch black. *This people group is too far gone, love too far forsaken, we thought. Let's go home, letting them come to us, on our terms and with our ways.* Somehow recollections of a vacant inn deterred us, however. Aromas of the stable, the story about laying down perfection for the sake of the stench, delivering presence to a rebelling culture. "I must leave my home," Christmas seemed to say, "and come to them, showing them the freedom of my Way."

....

This year I've been thinking about Jesus in his early thirties, about his vocation. I've been thinking about how just a few years into his ministry, Jesus laid down that ministry for the sake of a different one, a mass-of-Christ one, bleeding life into lives far beyond his humanity. I've been

---

17 Evagrius Ponticus, *The Praktikos.* Quoted in Kathleen Norris, Acedia & Me: A Marriage, Monks, and a Writer's Life (New York: Riverhead Books, 2010).

thinking about how humble, and inviting, and gloriously absurd that seems.

Dallas Willard said, "It was an important day in my life when at last I understood that if he needed forty days in the wilderness at one point, I very likely could use three or four."[18] I agree. Advent bears winter in its arms, I'm learning, but isn't overtaken by her. She bears the icy despair, but isn't frozen or crushed by it. Advent cradles the story of the savior, the boy giggling rowdily at rising dust from his wooden truck, the man who eventually paved dust's way Home. Advent knows sorrow and she knows sorrow's healer. She shares in the wicked death of winter, and pierces miraculous conception into winter's midst.

And in despair I bowed my head;

"There is no peace on earth," I said;

"For hate is strong,

And mocks the song

Of peace on earth, good-will to men!"

Then pealed the bells more loud and deep:

"God is not dead, nor doth He sleep;

The Wrong shall fail,

The Right prevail,

With peace on earth, good-will to men." [19]

No longer do I hate this season, and in fact, I quite savor five weeks of

---

18 Dallas Willard, *The Divine Conspiracy: Rediscovering Our Hidden Life in God* (San Francisco: Harper, 1998).
19 Henry Wadsworth Longfellow. "Christmas Bells," 1863.

permission to ponder the story of Jesus as fetus and toddler, friend and brother. I enjoy the intentional emphasis on a transcendent God choosing to become immanent, empathetically engaging in human hungers and longing. "Marry someone who's endlessly fascinating to you," a mentor once counseled. Likewise, I crave a God who's endlessly fascinating, who's winsome and gracious and never grows dull. I crave a God with whom I can share hunger and fatigue and bites of broiled fish. And I think I've found this God in Christmas.

As they were talking about these things, Jesus himself stood among them, and said to them, "Peace to you!" But they were startled and frightened and thought they saw a spirit. And he said to them, "Why are you troubled, and why do doubts arise in your hearts? See my hands and my feet, that it is I myself. Touch me, and see. For a spirit does not have flesh and bones as you see that I have." And when he had said this, he showed them his hands and his feet. And while they still disbelieved for joy and were marveling, he said to them, "Have you anything here to eat?" They gave him a piece of broiled fish, and he took it and ate before them.

—Luke 24:36–43

I've also decided this season doesn't hate me. "When it is dark enough, you can see the stars," Martin Luther King, Jr. said. Indeed, Christmas is not trying to mock my sorrows and make decorative light of my pain. Rather, it seeks to lighten my heavy load, speaking hope and presence where I'm still lonely, thoughtfully guiding me Home.

Today I shall seek to look my depression in the eye, to see it as a piece of my story, and to speak to it with peaceful separation from me: *I am not you, but I do struggle with your holds on me. My Father allowed, even ordained, darkness into this hour, that I might grow to see a bit more of him through it. To look a bit more like him. I am a daughter of Christ and the cleft of Christ's Word will be my refuge.*

> *They shall hunger no more, neither thirst anymore;*
> *the sun shall not strike them,*
> *nor any scorching heat.*

> *For the Lamb in the midst of the throne will be their shepherd,*
> *and he will guide them to springs of living water,*
> *and God will wipe away every tear from their eyes.*

> *—Revelation 7:16–17*

> *The Lord has said that he would dwell in thick darkness.*

> *—II Chronicles 6:1*

> *He uncovers the deeps out of darkness*
> *and brings deep darkness to light.*

> *—Job 12:22*

> *For it is you who light my lamp;*
> *the Lord my God lightens my darkness.*

> *—Psalm 18:28*

> *Even the darkness is not dark to you;*
> *the night is bright as the day,*
> *for darkness is as light with you.*

> *—Psalm 139:12*

> *I will give you the treasures of darkness*
> *and the hoards in secret places,*

that you may know that it is I, the LORD,
the God of Israel, who call you by your name…

I form light and create darkness;
I make well-being and create calamity;
I am the LORD, who does all these things.

—Isaiah 45:3; 7

But as for me, my prayer is to you, O LORD.
At an acceptable time, O God,

in the abundance of your steadfast love answer me in your saving
faithfulness.
Deliver me
from sinking in the mire;
let me be delivered from my enemies
and from the deep waters.

Let not the flood sweep over me,

or the deep swallow me up,
or the pit close its mouth over me.

Answer me, O LORD, for your steadfast love is good;
according to your abundant mercy, turn to me.
Hide not your face from your servant;
for I am in distress; make haste to answer me.

—Psalm 69:13–17

My flesh and my heart may fail,
but God is the strength of my heart and my portion forever.

—Psalm 73:26

*We are afflicted in every way, but not crushed; perplexed, but not driven to
despair; persecuted, but not forsaken; struck down, but not destroyed; always
carrying in the body the death of Jesus, so that the life of Jesus may also be
manifested in our bodies.*

—II Corinthians 4:8–10

*Rejoice not over me, O my enemy;
when I fall, I shall rise;
when I sit in darkness, the LORD will be a light to me.*

—Micah 7:8

*I waited patiently for the LORD;
he inclined to me and heard my cry.*

*He drew me up from the pit of destruction,
out of the miry bog,
and set my feet upon a rock,*

*making my steps secure.
He put a new song in my mouth,
a song of praise to our God.*

—Psalm 40:1–3a

*In the morning, O LORD, You will hear my voice; In the morning I will
order my prayer to You and eagerly watch.*

—Psalm 5:3 (NASB)

*My beloved speaks and says to me: "Arise, my love, my beautiful one, and
come away, for behold, the winter is past; the rain is over and gone. The
flowers appear on the earth, the time of singing has come, and the voice of
the turtledove is heard in our land. The fig tree ripens its figs, and the vines*

are in blossom; they give forth fragrance. Arise, my love, my beautiful one, and come away.

—*Song of Solomon 2:10-13*

···

We've been "trying" more intentionally these last few months, and to my jaw-dropping surprise, *it happened.* The stick showed two lines, not one. "TWO, NOT ONE!?" So much for diagnoses of endometriosis and past bouts with eating and exercise disorders preventing me from bearing babies. I intended to wait until he got home from work and concoct some imaginative way to tell him. Instead I dialed his number about three minutes after knowing.

Things have changed already. Not just bodily, but in realizing *it's not just me anymore;* I am more than just me. The small crew we've told have had a large crew of ideas and opinions. "Will you home-school, use cloth diapers, have a hospital or home-birth...?" I thought the wedding process came with a lot of commentary. Unfamiliar sensations bathed my torso yesterday when I opened an email addressed: "Mommy to be," a title so strong and life-giving, seemingly sacred beyond my reach.

4. FORM

"We are not taught much about the wilder aspects of Christianity. But these are what artists have wrestled with throughout the years. The Annunciation has been a favorite subject of painters and poets, because gestation and birth-giving are basic to any form of creation. All of us who have given birth to a baby, to a story, know that it is ultimately mystery, closely knit to God's own creative activities which did not stop at the beginning of the universe. God is constantly creating, in us, through us, with us, and to co-create with God is our human calling."

—Madeleine L'Engle, *Walking on Water: Reflections on Faith and Art*

Protestants have a weird fear about Jesus' mom, like we'll get cooties if we think about her too much, but I've been thinking much about Mary lately. Premarital pregnancy, being told by an angel not to sweat it because you're carrying the Savior—laboring with God, nursing him, marveling at his wobbly first steps. Eventually watching the boy you potty-trained bleed to death on a cross. Either these scenarios are a fantastic fable, or some of the most outrageous miracles to hit earth. And outrageous meditations on motherhood, which I'm obviously thinking about a lot these days, spurred on by matters such as my bellybutton disappearing.

It's true, and it looks odd. These months have done bizarre things to my psyche and more bizarre things to my body (or maybe it's vice versa). They've shaped new parts of me and apparently unshaped parts that were formerly known as me, like my naval. As of this unremarkable late summer Tuesday, the wrinkly crevice in my midsection has ebbed into flatness. After a few weeks of unfolding, it disappeared into nothingness, and looks odd. There's a part of me that wants to resist it, that wants it back. To reshape it into my old familiar belly button. But there's a part of me that doesn't.

Images of clay and the potter from the book of Isaiah have been coming to mind. "But now, O LORD, you are our Father; we are the clay, and you are our potter; we are all the work of your hand."[20] Clay is helpless by itself, and the potter is somehow not himself apart from the joy of his malleable canvas. So often I resist both sides of this, either running solo as the clay or buying into the illusion that I am the potter. So often I forget that I am clay, alongside an unfathomably creative and capable potter. Determined to shape, I forgo his mastery.

For instance with "envy," desiring beyond what I've been given, which has

---

20 Isaiah 64:8.

been strangling the life out of me this week. Jesus' brother said, "where jealousy and selfish ambition exist, there will be disorder and every vile practice."[21] I've felt this pandemonium and practice counseling me toward resentment—toward dissatisfaction with my place in God's order of creation.

Part of it may be the mommy wars thing. Without even having a baby beyond the womb stage, I've found the amount of warring between rightness and wrongness in the realm of raising tykes wildly overwhelming. We put so many expectations on our stories, and on our babies' stories, and our families' stories, leaving us mean and cold and guarded. I was with a friend the other day who was discussing her views of homeschooling and how they differ from other friends, which she'd reduced to a differing value system—in essence, she was communicating that her way was right, and any other way fell below it. My guess is, those "other friends" have at times deduced this friend's views as weird, or isolated, or even less virtuous. We're just so hard on ourselves and on each other, no? We concoct these add-on commandments that were never intended to carry inherent moral value.

Pursuits of excellence and grace don't seem to naturally merge. "Think about the most important people in your life," my friend Juli's pediatrician said at her son's first appointment. "Who has had the greatest impact on you? Now... which of them was breastfed?" He went on to encourage her efforts to nurse her son, knowing it's important, but he also wanted to emphasize that she hasn't failed as a mom if barriers prevent her from being able to nurse.

We've got clusters of friends we "do life with" in some shape or form, but we inwardly think they have wrong values, or at least that ours are more

---

21 James 3:16.

right. Whether vaccines or breastfeeding, Mozart or cloth diapering, Pitocin or organic... When all the while there are upwards of 150 million children[22] with no available home, mommy, school, vaccines, diapers, or healthcare. At all. And we keep ranting about our first world issues and friends with value differences and strollers that don't roll straight.

Jesus taught that we must go *beyond* the righteousness of the scribes and the Pharisees.[23] I don't suppose he was belittling righteousness altogether, as the seriousness with which this crowd took God-following was beyond compare. But it was also neurotically *external*. "The extent to which we have gone beyond the righteousness of the scribes and the Pharisees," then, says Richard Foster, "is seen in how much our lives demonstrate the internal work of God upon the heart."[24] Apparently our children, and their behavior and health and wealth and happiness, has an inappropriate hold on us—an idolatry in us.

It dawned on me recently that Adam and Eve strayed, and their dad was God. Clearly there's a breakdown for us modern folks. If parenting is about producing top-notch children, we're all up a creek without a paddle. Among other reasons, "top-notch" is subjective and varies significantly by person, region, country, and continent. My friend Claudia, a psychologist for thirty years, reminded me today that God doesn't have grandchildren. In other words, when all is said and done, he's the primary caretaker. Our kids can be the most well-versed, polite, healthy, strong, brave, and well-behaved, but if their hearts never surrender to the Father's love, *all other ground is sinking sand*. Mindful parenting, I'm learning, is about pointing souls toward Jesus, not promising their wellness or salvation.

---

22 "Statistics," *Christian Alliance for Orphans*, accessed June 9, 2017, https://cafo.org/ovc/statistics.
23 See Matthew 5:20.
24 Richard Foster, *Celebration of Discipline: The Path to Spiritual Growth* (New York: Harper Collins, 1978), 9.

Sometimes I wonder how much of our mommy warring rests in our own insecurity—our own fears of being seen in our weakness, exposed in our failure. If only we can paint a reflection of ourselves (via our children) that's noteworthy and valuable, we too, shall feel noteworthy and valuable. Consider the account of teenage Mary in Luke 1. Likely in her first trimester with the Son of God, she traveled about seventy miles from Nazareth to visit Elizabeth, an elderly relative who was pregnant with John the Baptist. Maybe it was refreshing for Mary to share time with someone beyond her teenage wisdom. Likewise, Elizabeth had had quite a miraculous conception herself, which I imagine was an encouragement to Mary in further accepting her own unbelievable account.

But put yourself in Elizabeth's shoes. Might you have felt a twinge of envy? *Why did Mary get to be pregnant right after puberty (versus menopause), while she endured prayer and obedience and barrenness for decade after decade after decade? Why did Mary get to look young and lovely with "the pregnancy glow," while Elizabeth withered away in fat and wrinkles and with a husband who couldn't even talk anymore? Surely Elizabeth was grateful for her pregnancy, but wouldn't it have made better sense for her, not a teen, to carry the really special son? Hadn't God heard this faithful Jewish woman's desires to be the Messiah's mother?* Apart from the grace of the Holy Spirit, yes, these thoughts probably would've been Elizabeth's. But look instead at how she responds:

> *And when Elizabeth heard the greeting of Mary, the baby leaped in her womb. And Elizabeth was filled with the Holy Spirit, and she exclaimed with a loud cry, "Blessed are you among women, and blessed is the fruit of your womb! And why is this granted to me that the mother of my Lord should come to me? For behold, when the sound of your greeting came to my ears, the baby in my womb leaped for joy. And blessed is she who believed*

that there would be a fulfillment of what was spoken to her from the Lord.[25]

From a human standpoint, Elizabeth *should've* envied Mary. Instead, she was able to celebrate and affirm her arrival, and the arrival of the Messiah. Elizabeth's heart rejoiced with this unborn child, already referring to Jesus' embryo as "my Lord." (And her own embryo, John the Baptist, leapt with worshipful joy at the sound of Mary's voice.) She counts herself *honored* that God would choose her to share this news with and goes on to affirm Mary, saying *And blessed is she who believed that.*

The Bible talks about a foe who wars against us day in and day out,[26] purposed to steal, kill and destroy[27] that which is good about us and our days. If he can get to us to believe what we're desiring is dissatisfactory, or too weird, or gross, or unheard of to say out loud, he's done his job. Envy causes us to lose contentment in God and in who God has made each of us to be. Its roots lie in unbelief, while its repellant is trust. "Love," however, "is patient and kind,"[28] so "Don't be wishing you were someplace else or with someone else. Where you are right now is God's place for you."[29]

Naked I came from my mother's womb, and naked shall I return. The LORD gave, and the LORD has taken away; blessed be the name of the LORD.

—Job 1:21

It's but 9 a.m., and a corner of my heart is sickened and exhausted by political jargon. The bullying, the hatred, the anger—it feels like we're in middle school. Another corner of my heart is consumed by the small

25 Luke 1:41–45.
26 See Ephesians 6:11–13.
27 See John 10:10.
28 I Corinthians 13:4a
29 I Corinthians 7:17, The Message Translation

human growing in my abdomen. There's joy and anticipation, and there's fear and ambiguity. I ponder Mary those final days before delivery, worn by months of pregnancy and unsure whether she could make it. I feel her weariness. Reaching down, I massage the smooth skin of my naval, pondering complexities it held just days ago. Pondering clay and my Potter's wheel, stretching, molding, forming, his delicate kiln causing some of me to disappear, that room might be made for a new creation.

The midwife reminded me at our last appointment, "Though you know nearly nothing about how these final weeks will unfold, your baby and your body know them exactly." Maybe this is similar to what Paul said in his first letter to Corinth: "Just think—you don't need a thing, you've got it all! All God's gifts are right in front of you as you wait expectantly for our Master Jesus to arrive on the scene for the Finale. And not only that, but God himself is right alongside to keep you steady and on track until things are all wrapped up by Jesus. God, who got you started in this spiritual adventure, shares with us the life of his Son and our Master Jesus. He will never give up on you. Never forget that."[30]

Father, in the midst of life's contractions today, please help me cling to your relentless love. Thank you that you don't get anxious. You aren't surprised or caught off guard by things, like I am. Please "Say to my soul, 'I am your salvation!'"[31] and I am your unborn child's salvation. Unshackle me from believing such liberty can come from any other source or name.

---

30 I Corinthians 1:7–9, MSG.
31 Psalm 35:3b.

5. WORTH

I wonder how many people I've looked at all my life and never seen.

—John Steinbeck, The Winter of Our Discontent

If God gives such attention to the appearance of wildflowers—most of which are never even seen—don't you think he'll attend to you, take pride in you, do his best for you?

—Matthew 6:30 (MSG)

Every passing April I remember the last time, seven years ago now. Hunched over the bathtub, my middle finger jabbed the familiar spot in my throat, puking up remnants from my pantry and cake leftover from a gathering. Oh and ice cream, probably the hundredth pint I'd bought, convincing myself at the counter, "this time will be different—this time I'll eat in moderation, just like all the diet experts and websites and magazines say I can." But a moderate amount led to another horrifying binge on all the "bad food" in the vicinity of my apartment.

Eating struggles began gnawing at me around age twelve. It was the era of fat free, when my mom swore by pretzels and Diet Coke and lusted in misery over her size six reflection. I began running and kept a detailed journal of all fat grams that invaded my body. A year later found me significantly underweight, religious in my diet and daily three mile run. Anorexia had grabbed me by the throat.

High school brought a new load of social pressures and academic striving. Controlling my calories and exercise provided stability and confidence. Weighing less furthered me as a distance runner and didn't seem to affect my tennis rankings. Outsiders even seemed to admire my thinness and discipline. Little did they know I worshiped them. My parents saw through it and sent me to a therapist, but I was unwanting of help. My gods were my body and food, and no one, I determined, would come in the way of them.

Playing college-level tennis a couple years later, strength and weight training preached their way into my paradigm. I bulked up and now began controlling my fears by overeating. With the team or classmates in the cafeteria I would eat healthily, then binge on "bad food" when alone. Everything had a category, and every day's scorecard boiled down to caloric and exercise intakes.

Running mileage increased, as did attempts at vegetarian, vegan, raw, and gluten-free regimens. Downtime was spent studying my sacraments of food and health. As well as trying to learn about this new identity I'd awakened to as "God's daughter." Honestly, I was just as harsh and unforgiving with myself after becoming a Christian. Jesus-following folks simply considered me the healthy athlete girl who never ate sugar and always stayed in shape. It's sad to me that this personality gets by so easily. I was head-deep in a battle with addictions to food and body and self.

Years passed, compulsive overeating met purging, and they became pals. I became bulimic, publicly consuming normal portions of healthy meals, plus massive portions of "bad," "unhealthy" foods in seclusion. Unlike anorexia and its outward signs, bulimia led me into a hidden love affair with food. Support groups helped, as did prayer, books, roommates, and letting go of things like mirrors, television, and perusing celebrity images in magazines and online, but the fight toward wellness was still a daily battle, a battle that many days I lost. Being an "author," or "in seminary," or "serving overseas as a missionary" only heaped more shame at my doorstep. "You know better… should be better than this… beyond that… different from who you are." These were ever-present voices. The majority of my conversations with God felt like they related to food and body. Though his response, or my healing, seemed negligible, even absent at times, I had to trust I was moving. And believe he was too.

My fourth counselor explained bulimia as a bridge. "You don't have the language for what's going on in your heart yet, Abbie," I heard her say in a tone that was truthful, though not judgmental, and gave me the option of whether or not to believe her. "Maybe this disease is a gateway to new ways of learning to love yourself and God." The idea that my issues could be a bridge of sorts sounded outlandish and out of sync with the ways I knew at present. It also sounded too wonderful to be true. Could God really take my diseased and dead parts and bridge them into something lovely?

The Spirit didn't snap his fingers and heal me, but something did snap inside me, catapulting a new leg of my healing. For one, I started being nice to myself, and further differentiating between my true self, loved and designed by a thoughtful Maker, and my eating disorder. I started believing maybe God meant it when he said, "you are precious in my eyes, and honored, and I love you."[32] When loading-up my "binge cart" at the grocery store, I would tell it what a bully and liar it was, and how it may not seem the case in this moment, but Jesus would be victorious here. "Even in this weak place," I would preach to myself, "he is at work." My identity shifted from a sinner who's saved to a saint who struggles at times with sin. I began to believe Gerald May that "To be alive is to be addicted, and to be alive and addicted is to stand in need of grace."[33]

Slowly I started coming out of hiding, learning to call safe friends after I'd messed up and eventually in the midst of the mess. I found permission to be more freedom-filled than restrictive. When I want to eat chocolate cake now, I do. When I don't want to exercise, I don't. And I'm learning to accept that if exercise isn't acting as an idol for me, a healthy and growing amount of squish and cellulite and wrinkle will bless my frame each passing year. I try to avoid labels of "bad" and "good" and simply eat foods that are tasty and make me feel alive. And unlike the years where food and I shared a mostly private table and conversation, most meals

---

32 Isaiah 43:4a.
33 *Addiction and Grace: Love and Spirituality in the Healing of Addictions*, (San Francisco: Harper Collins Publishers, 1988), 11.

now enjoy the company of others. In the words of C.S. Lewis, "God never meant man to be a purely spiritual creature. That is why he uses material things like bread and wine to put the new life into us. We may think that is rather crude and unspiritual. God does not; he invented eating. He likes matter. He invented it."[34] I actually believe this now.

....

A couple nights ago I posted a status about going to dinner with neighbors who are black. I mentioned how it felt to be the only one of my color at the table, and how much I have to learn about being the minority.

"Just curious," Micah posed from beside me on the couch, "Why did you just post that?"

"I don't know... I mean, they're true sentiments... but... I don't know..."

I unposted it, unsure why my hand felt like it was half-way down the cookie jar. Something about his inquiry was stirring, startling. Why did I post it? What did I want to tell you by these words?

So much of what I do and don't do I'm realizing is about my image.

Protecting it.

Preserving it.

Molding it.

---

34 C.S. Lewis, *The Complete C.S. Lewis Signature Classics* (Grand Rapids, MI : Zondervan, 2007), 60.

To look like ___.

So someone thinks ___.

Or to appear like ___?

So someone doesn't think ___.

Part of me was genuinely honored to dine with a table racially different from me; I know heaven's dinners will be like that. And I genuinely wanted all my "friends" to know about it. I believe in equality and social justice and the fight against racism, in my soul and social life and neighborhood. By a simple question, however, layers beneath became genuinely obvious—layers that motivate letters on a screen to formulate a sentence and a story for the whole world to see—to formulate an image about me and what I'm living for, and what you should think about me because of it—that what I do is good. Because deep down I want you to think I'm good and likable and worth loving.

Deep down, I want you to think I have a life. Not a boring life. I want you to think I do interesting things on Tuesday nights. Interesting and virtuous. I want you to have a certain impression of our marriage. That we value meaningful things. And are humble. And love our neighbors. And do justice. Because that would make us admirable. And social justice is sexy right now. Deep down, I want you to think I live a certain way. And am insecure at the thought of you thinking I don't. Or insecure at the thought of thinking that I don't. Deep down, I want to control my image.

Seems like we Jesus-followers seldom believe what God says about us. And not knowing we're his beloved means we'll fight to death to become someone else's. Mary knew her baby was God. But instead of shouting that seemingly good truth from the rooftops, she chose to "treasure up these truths, pondering them in her heart."[35] As if they were a brilliant secret between she and God. Maybe it was. And maybe it wasn't her job to convince the world of the truth, even if it affected her image. Maybe it wasn't her job to control the truths the world believed. Her job was to steward, to carry, to bear life—ultimately bearing witness to the light within. "For God, who said, 'Let light shine out of darkness,' has shone in our hearts to give the light of the knowledge of the glory of God in the face of Jesus Christ."[36]

....

Our friend Gracie came for chicken chili and my mucus plug unplugged. From start to finish, the birth process was back labor. The mean nurse told me at four centimeters, "This is nothing; just wait." The night shift nurse was kind and breathed with me through a tidal wave contraction. Calmly afterward, as if a prophetic word offered in confident humility, she said, "Second to breathing, birthing a baby is the most natural process to which a woman can give herself. Let this move beyond you."

Reminds me of our virgin wedding night, maybe, clueless as to two becoming one. At some point our bodies moved beyond us, graciously taking over. As if a most natural process, love knew a way we didn't.

Another tidal wave bulldozed through my back.

"If one feels the need for something grand," Vincent Van Gogh said, "something infinite, something that makes one feel more aware of God,

---

35 See Luke 2:19.
36 II Corinthians 4:6.

one need not go far to find it. I think I see something deeper, more infinite, more eternal than the ocean in the expression of the eyes of a little baby when it wakes in the morning, and coos or laughs because it sees the sun shining on its cradle."[37] Indeed.

An hour of pushes later, unglamorously seated on the birthing stool positioned against the porcelain toilet, a body sprang forth from mine. Almost as if too sacred for words, Micah whispered, "It's a girl," as the midwife laid her moist, delicate body in my arms.

They say you fall madly in love that moment, and the previous excruciating moments are suddenly forgotten. Thankfully my friend Nicole had forewarned me that sometimes this isn't true, that sometimes falling in love takes time. The placenta passed and a nurse I'd never seen helped me put on a diaper. In high school I remember trying on homecoming dresses, sheepish about my mom seeing me unclothed. She told me I needed to get over it, that someday I'd have a baby and everyone would see everything. Someday and I were now acquainted.

Analytically, we had known "the whole creation has been groaning together in the pains of childbirth until now."[38] Now we knew experientially. Her birth story felt naïve and miraculous and fierce, as if to proclaim to the world the etymology of her name. Elliana: though our ground has Fallen, our God has responded.

Four days after she was born, Micah was doing taxes and eating cashews at the kitchen table. He nonchalantly inquired whether we should get prenatal coverage again. I wept. The weight of the Fall remained palpable and terrifying. "Never again—I cannot bear the birthing process again."

---

37 Vincent Van Gogh to Theo Van Gogh, 10 December 1882. *Vincent Van Gogh: The Letters*, accessed June 9, 2017, http://vangoghletters.org/vg/letters/let292/letter.html.
38 Romans 8:22.

The sounds of the groan were gripping and intimate.

So much about life seems traumatic. But so much about the Gospel story—the "Good News" of Jesus story—does too. It seems traumatic and confusing, unearthing and unknown, while somehow pregnant with a majestic glory, safely tucked in a womb of provision. Maybe labor embodies a union with the sufferings of Jesus. Maybe it's a form of communion—his body, stretched and broken for mine, torn and poured out for the sake of my birth—and now, my body, stretched and broken, torn and poured out for the sake of this beloved bundle sleeping in my arms.

Thus says the Lord God to these bones: Behold, I will cause breath to enter you, and you shall live. And I will lay sinews upon you, and will cause flesh to come upon you, and cover you with skin, and put breath in you, and you shall live, and you shall know that I am the Lord.

—Ezekiel 37:5–6

A Collect for the Presence of Christ

Lord Jesus, stay with us, for evening is at hand and the day is past; be our companion in the way, kindle our hearts, and awaken hope, that we may know thee as thou art revealed in Scripture and the breaking of bread. Grant this for the sake of thy love. Amen.[39]

---

39 "Evening Collect from the Book of Common Prayer," *Book of Common Prayer Online,* accessed June 6, 2017, http://www.bcponline.org/DailyOffice/ep1.html.

6. MARKED

To pray is to descend with the mind into the heart, and there to stand before the face of the Lord, ever-present, all-seeing, within you.[40]

—*Theophan the Recluse, Russian Mystic*

I bless the LORD *who gives me counsel;*
in the night also my heart instructs me.

—*Psalm 16:7*

---

40 Timothy Ware, ed., *The Art of Prayer: An Orthodox Anthology* (London: Faber & Faber, 1966), 110.

They were moments packed with shame, and sobs, and fearful regret that one day she would know. I wasn't prepared for how Elliana would look, or develop. Apparently I wasn't prepared for what happens when you move a watermelon through a bean hole (and weren't exactly gracious toward the watermelon in the process).

She looked squished when she came out. She was puffy, with pinched eyes and a red face. When she screamed, her features crinkled together like aluminum foil. I laid in bed one of those first nights, exhausted and hormonally still massively pregnant.

"Everyone said when they laid her on my chest I'd think she was the most gorgeous human being to bless the planet." Cue ugly crying. "But I don't think our daughter is beautiful." More crying.

It crushed me. How could I be so cruel? So vain? So abusive toward God's creative workmanship? "For you formed her inward parts; you knitted her together in my womb. I praise you, for she is fearfully and wonderfully made. Wonderful are your works; my soul knows it very well."[41] I wanted my soul to know this, but it didn't.

I'm smitten with Elliana's beauty now and could stare at her all day long. It's increasingly been this way since soon after my low, revelatory night. It changed me. She changed me. Her ivory skin and lips, soft and smooth, and brown eyes "that could take over Europe with their strength," her uncle once said. I'm diverging and missing my point though. By ironing out and justifying why I wasn't smitten with her beauty and now am, I've begun to objectify beauty. I've begun to fit it into a box that "isn't" at this point, and then "becomes" at this point. But that's not how beauty works. It runs deeper, and deeper still.

---

41 Paraphrased from Psalm 139:13–14.

Now she's three months old and an acne factory, and I am becoming less vain. The double chin and oozing eyes and shedding skin now strike me as healthy phases of newborn development. But it's hard for me to let go of those early tears, those critical thoughts that she wasn't beautiful. What was this based on? What is beauty based on? I believe it vital to a female's livelihood to know at a core level that she is beautiful. Where do I go from here?

Easily perceived as beautiful now, what might happen when Elliana leaves the cute toddler stage and hits middle school, or adolescence; puberty and pudgy aren't beautiful in our culture. What happens when she's overweight, or overly pale, or underweight, or so many other unacceptable variables? What happens when she has too many freckles, or pimples, or scars, or hairs? Or too little of something? What happens when she gets leukemia and goes bald, or hit by a car and must amputate her legs? How then will we explore with her understandings of beauty? How now do I explore with myself understandings of beauty, devastatingly aware that though I inform or instruct Elliana one way, should she watch me perform and insult my beauty in another, that will be the instruction she imbibes most readily and deeply.

Years into marriage, it's still weird to me that Micah likes my shapely thighs and overabundance of freckles. You don't want to know how many hours of my twenties were spent trying to hide these seemingly hideous aspects of myself. Some cavernous part of me believed God shaped my shapely thighs and thoughtfully crafted my skin type, but they were still horrifying and seemed the reason, most days, that I was single, or shouldn't wear cute pants. Had I known now what I didn't then, so many of my years would've been less fretful. Nevertheless, when I'm standing naked in the bathroom, bloated and with more wrinkles and dimples and grays than my posted photos reveal—when morning breath and body odor and tired eyes are my radiance—how might he answer my sleepless question: "Honey, do you think I'm beautiful?"

Rarely do I have the guts to ask such a question. At some level, I'm too afraid of the answer. At a deeper level, the grace of tears arrives. In the moment everything feels like "no." Deeper, still, I know the answer is yes. "My darling, we're here again aren't we?" he'll say. "I know you don't feel this way, but it's true. It's the unchanging truth." Beauty's story must have more depth than its cover; I must have more depth than my cover. In order to mother my darling well, I must have the courage to dig deeper with her, and with myself, into these inner pages. "Charm is deceitful, and beauty is vain, but a woman who fears the LORD is to be praised."[42] Fine, let it flee, but I still want it, and want it for my daughter. Is this bad? Maybe it's not bad, but I think it's fragile. If beauty doesn't have a deeper foundation than ivory skin and a skinny body, it's bound to fail, and frustrate, and foster resentment toward one's self and Maker. "Do not let your adorning be external," the apostle Peter says, "the braiding of hair and the putting on of gold jewelry, or the clothing you wear—but let your adorning be the hidden person of the heart with the imperishable beauty of a gentle and quiet spirit, which in God's sight is very precious."[43]

"Gentle and quiet" often ticks gals off, especially those of us who aren't always gentle or quiet. Honestly, the words don't budge much through

---

42 Proverbs 31:30.
43 I Peter 3:3-6.

different translations, but I quite prefer "meek," as told by the King James Version. To me, it implies humility and submission, the laying down of one's life (as referenced in the next verse). It implies Christlikeness. Christ, who made and mirrors beauty—me, with Christ dwelling within, mirroring beauty to the world—my daughter, beautiful because she's made in the Image of Beauty.

....

March 13th. Kevin and Meagan came for pizza and Elliana cried through most of it. Something roared in me inwardly, wanting her to stop. Maybe it was from embarrassment that "this was our new normal"? Then I wondered if they really think she's cute, or just said so because everyone says that about newborns. I'm so sorry, Father. To grapple with discontents at my body seems okay, but to do so with her—I just hate it. The pride and vanity and performance issues being exposed in my heart—ugh. I long to mother with a purity of heart that doesn't seek to control outcomes or beauty. Help me steward this child well, this season well, continuing to open my heart to your healing graces. Guard her from direct hits of my sin, and as they do hit her, keep me coming back to your forgiveness and love.

As if peacefully aware of her beauty this morning, Elliana stared contentedly into the stainless refrigerator. Oh how I long for this acceptance to last. But I know better. I know it will soon become tainted, the truth of her reflection and true self growing increasingly difficult to see. What is my role in that as her mother? Am I permitting space for vulnerable conversations and explorations of her body and sexuality? Am I permitting space for my own vulnerable conversations and explorations of my body and sexuality with God?

My journal shows a list of body parts scribed during one of last night's feedings. Initially I remember they birthed prayers over her; soon I realized they were over me, as well, over our strong and delicate frames, our hope to live today in the bodies God has crafted for us and marked as his own.

Mirrors: It's daunting to realize what I see in the mirror is what you will learn to see, too. May mirrors not play a larger role in our lives than they need to. For now we see in a mirror dimly, but then face to face. Now I know in part; then I shall know fully, even as I have been fully known.[44] This glass is but a dim reflection meant to mirror the Image of God in us. May we search for that Image, dear daughter, in ourselves and in others.

Hair: When it changes, grows, falls out, thins, do not dismay. Gray hair is a crown of glory; it is gained in a righteous life.[45] Even to your old age he is God; to gray hairs he will carry you. He has made, and he will bear; he will carry and will save.[46] As it is brushed and cleaned and caressed, may you sense the dignity and precision by which you've been made, every last hair of your head numbered and known.[47]

Eyes: They're an incredible lens in which to see the abundance of creation. May color and movement and intricacy astound you. Your eyes will also tempt and tell you you're ugly at times, undesirable and to be hidden.[48] Search for the eyes of the Lord in your midst, which are ever searching to strengthen hearts committed to Him.[49] He opens the eyes of the blind[50] and enlightens the eyes of our hearts that we may know what is the hope to which we've been called.[51] May you have eyes to see the truth, about

---

44 See I Corinthians 13:12.
45 Proverbs 16:31.
46 See Isaiah 46:4.
47 See Luke 12:7.
48 See Genesis 3:6–7.
49 See II Chronicles 16:9.
50 Psalm 146:8.
51 See Ephesians 1:18.

yourself, God, and the world around you today.

Nose: May you remember its blessings, eliciting smells of crayons and spaghetti, campfires and freshly cut grass. Thanks be to God, who always leads us in triumph in Christ, and manifests through us the sweet aroma of the knowledge of him.[52] Some have noses, but do not smell.[53] Oh daughter, may you smell deeply today the aromas of Christ.

Ears: The Lord said, "Go out and stand on the mountain in the presence of the LORD, for the LORD is about to pass by." Then a great and powerful wind tore the mountains apart and shattered the rocks before the Lord, but the Lord was not in the wind. After the wind there was an earthquake, but the Lord was not in the earthquake. After the earthquake came a fire, but the Lord was not in the fire. And after the fire came a gentle whisper.[54] May this be the whisper you spend your days waiting and wanting to hear. This is the voice you were made for.

Mouth: Open your mouth wide, and he will fill it, daughter.[55] Do not be afraid of man, for God is with you to deliver you. He will speak for you; he will put words in your mouth.[56] You have been given a unique voice and song and tone of laughter. Your story is worth listening to. May you speak it with courage.

Face: It tells a stunning story, unlike any told in all the earth. When you become ashamed of how you look, pause to remember the eyes of the Lord looking upon you. May he bless you and keep you; the Lord make his face to shine upon you and be gracious to you; the Lord lift up his

---

52 See II Corinthians 2:14.
53 Psalm 115:6. 54 I Kings 19:11–12, New International Version.
54 I Kings 19:11–12, New International Version.
55 See Psalm 81:10.
56 See Jeremiah 1:6–9.

countenance upon you and give you peace.[57] Those who look to him are radiant, and their faces shall never be ashamed.[58] Child, your beauty runs deeper than you know.

Mind: It will be attacked, accused, demeaned, and disturbed. May you guard it in Christ. Your mind is also an incredible vessel of worship. May you cultivate it in Christ. One of the Pharisees asked, "Teacher, which is the great commandment in the Law?" And Jesus said to him, "You shall love the Lord your God with all your heart and with all your soul and with all your mind. This is the great and first commandment."[59] May God open your mind to understand the Scriptures.[60] May he set your mind on things that are above, not on things that are on earth.[61] May you trust and fix your mind on him, for it is he who keeps you in perfect peace.[62]

Arms: "And he sat down and called the twelve. And he said to them, 'If anyone would be first, he must be last of all and servant of all.' And he took a child and put him in the midst of them, and taking him in his arms, he said to them, 'Whoever receives one such child in my name receives me, and whoever receives me, receives not me but him who sent me.'"[63] Be held often by the arms of Jesus.

Hands: And Jesus said to them, "Why are you troubled, and why do doubts arise in your hearts? See my hands and my feet, that it is I myself. Touch me, and see."[64] May you touch the truth more deeply than I. May you be humble and open-handed in your opinions, while clinging tightly to convicted beliefs. May your hands create widely and give generously

---

57 See Numbers 6:24–26.
58 Psalm 34:5.
59 See Matthew 22:34–40; 22:46; Luke 10:25–28.
60 See Luke 24:45.
61 See Colossians 3:2.
62 See Isaiah 26:3.
63 Mark 9:35–37.
64 Luke 24:38–39.

and bless abundantly.

Stomach: Food is a gift from your Father, to sustain and to nourish, to energize and to be enjoyed. When you are tempted to stuff and fill to escape the world's pains, may you remember he is with you. May you know he alone can fill. May you taste and see him in his glorious goodness.[65]

Chest: A sign of femininity and nourishment, of God's creativity toward the finale of creation. May you grow to dress it with the breastplate of righteousness. "You are he who took me from the womb; you made me trust you at my mother's breasts. On you was I cast from my birth, and from my mother's womb you have been my God."[66] As I have the blessing of nursing you, may you carry that blessing of nursing others with the bounty of Christ.

Knees: You crawled under the breakfast table this morning, finding grandeur in the chairs and thick wooden legs. You fiddled with my ankles. Hands cradled beneath your soft armpits, I returned you to the world above. You were proud and well postured, as if knowing you'd been invited to a table of the Lord. Maybe it was like the look when you're in your Papa's arms, cradled by the nook behind your chubby knees, beaming a story that says, "All is right." May you maintain this wonder for the world, growing to understand it as your Father's. May you kneel often.

Legs: Thoughtful bases of your body. Layered, squishy, and adorable now, someday you will likely abhor them. When hatred starts to fester, saying they're too shapely, or thick, or boney, recall the lengths to which these parts have taken you, the movement, the strength, crawling, standing,

---

65 See Psalm 34:8.
66 Psalm 22:9–10.

walking, jumping, skipping, dancing and kneeling. May your legs lead you into eternity, dear daughter, with the boldness, endurance and masterful beauty with which they've been made. "How beautiful are your feet in sandals," though, "O noble daughter! Your rounded thighs are like jewels, the work of a master hand."[67]

Feet: Too often we cover them. We forget how intricate and helpful and powerful they are. Let Christ wash your feet, then go and wash others'.[68] How beautiful are the feet of him who brings good news.[69] May your feet take you to unimaginable places of adventure, joy, and communion. And when you think, "My foot is slipping," know that his steadfast love will hold you up.[70]

Body: May your body be a temple of the Holy Spirit, whom God alone gives, realizing you are not your own but bought with a price.[71] Your body has enormous worth. It does not define you, daughter, but is a thoughtful expression of God's image. May you not abuse, or curse, or compete against your body, and may you learn worth enough in yourself to resist others' abuse. May you bless, care for, and partner with your body, recognizing it as a grounding vessel guiding you toward home.

My frame was not hidden from you,
when I was being made in secret,
intricately woven in the depths of the earth.
Your eyes saw my unformed substance;
in your book were written, every one of them,
the days that were formed for me,
when as yet there was none of them.

—Psalm 139:15–16

---

67 Song of Solomon 7:1.
68 See John 13:14.
69 See Isaiah 52:7 and Romans 10:15.
70 See Psalm 94:18.
71 See I Corinthians 6:19–20.

7. NEIGHBOR

We may be surprised at the people we find in heaven. God has a soft spot

for sinners. His standards are quite low.

—Desmond Tutu, South African social rights activist
and retired Anglican bishop

Guests have been visiting, some for an evening, some for a week, and one for two and a half weeks. I've loved it and I've cursed it. They've added energy and tones of laughter, perspectives on politics and how to chop an onion. They've also added opinions I could've survived without, plus they've unearthed my tendency to entertain.

> **en-ter-tain** [en-ter-teyn] – verb
> 1. to hold the attention of pleasantly or agreeably; divert; amuse.[72]

The thought of guests awakens this drive in me, to hold people's attention, or dutifully assure their amused well-being. That admission feels silly, if not impossible, when I write it out, yet still compelling. Particularly because my aim to perfect entertaining comes at the cost of being with and participating in the lives of whoever I'm with. In healthy hours, I remember that guests are a gift to be hosted, not a short-lived presence to be entertained—that simplicity and minimalism are treasures in the chest of human longing, and actual presence with another human being is a rare gem and marked diversion. Hospitality, that is.

> **hos-pi-tal-i-ty** [hos-pi-tal-i-tee] – noun
> 1. the friendly reception and treatment of guests or strangers
> 2. the quality or disposition of receiving and treating guests and strangers in a warm, friendly, generous way.[73]

When's the last time you hosted a stranger, or prepared for the quality of how you received and treated your guests? Me neither. "Do not neglect to show hospitality to strangers," the writer of Hebrews says, "for thereby some have entertained angels unawares."[74] Furthermore, we're to be hospitable without grumbling, thereby contributing to one another's needs.[75] I've grumbled a lot these weeks.

---

72 Dictionary.com (http://www.dictionary.com/browse/entertain, accessed September 13, 2017).
73 *Ibid.*
74 Hebrews 13:2.
75 See I Peter 4:9 and Romans 12:13.

Hospitality, it seems, insists on vulnerability and bids us to prioritize intimacy and presence—to open the doors of our home, even when the offering feels menial, burnt, or still dirty in the sink. "True hospitality," writes Kathleen Norris, "is marked by an open response to the dignity of each and every person."[76] Maybe you've heard the following story about Mary and Martha:

> *As they continued their travel, Jesus entered a village. A woman by the name of Martha welcomed him and made him feel quite at home. She had a sister, Mary, who sat before the Master, hanging on every word he said. But Martha was pulled away by all she had to do in the kitchen. Later, she stepped in, interrupting them. "Master, don't you care that my sister has abandoned the kitchen to me? Tell her to lend me a hand."*
>
> *The Master said, "Martha, dear Martha, you're fussing far too much and getting yourself worked up over nothing. One thing only is essential, and Mary has chosen it—it's the main course, and won't be taken from her."[77]*

I used to think these passages were about contemplative living and persuading me to fill out a monastery application (a legit consideration at points in my life). Now I think it's more about stewardship of time and utmost aims of hospitality and worship. More about Brother Lawrence's words that "We ought not to be weary of doing little things for the love of God, who regards not the greatness of the work, but the love with which it is performed."[78] Now I think Luke 10 is more about inviting me to prioritize Christ in all things, including work and hospitality.

Entertaining is not all bad, I'm learning, but it's also a fragile good. Jesus doesn't like me more when my marinara sauce is organic, or my floorboards

---

76 Kathleen Norris, *Dakota: A Spiritual Geography* (New York: Houghton Mifflin Company, 1993), 197.75 Luke 10:38–42, MSG.

77 Luke 10:38–42, MSG.

78 Brother Lawrence, *The Practice of the Presence of God* (Springdale, PA: Whitaker House, 1982), 22.

aren't dressed in dust. He likes me because he likes me. I've not read it, but I love the title of Mary Randolph Carter's book: *A Perfectly Kept House Is the Sign of a Misspent Life*. A clean home and unique centerpiece and tasty food are meaningful graces, but too often divert into expectations on ourselves, drawing attention away from the relational and toward the external, aiming for a meticulous facade that's pretty and put together, but fails to satisfy us deep down.

....

Yesterday I came upon a stranger on our porch—a guest, I knew Jesus would call her. She relaxed in the papasan, the puffy one with a soft, protective hold. Birds sang their lauds. It warms a gal's heart to see her home being used in this way, or it should. What about if she slept there, though? Or was homeless and had lived on the streets for four years, likely without a shower for four weeks? Would your heart stay warm when you saw thick mucus from her coughs, swollen veins from dialysis and years of drug use? Or when she told you she's thirty-six, with five kids (the oldest twenty-one), all taken away by Division of Family and Children Services? Would your heart stay warm when you saw her drool stains on your chair? Mine didn't.

Generally, I enjoy having guests. I enjoy learning about hospitality and what it means to host well, with open arms and an open heart. Yesterday reminded me I enjoy easy guests though—the tidy, healthy, ambitious, educated, helpful kind. The sick, dying, dirty, brokenhearted ones are a different story and don't fit the gospels I usually abide in, like security and prosperity, intellect and safety, health, wealth, and comfort.

Sometimes I wonder why God has us living in this neighborhood, where it's commonplace for the drunk neighbor to show on our doorstep, belligerent for money. Or to watch from the front window as a prostitute walks into Leon's house. *Shouldn't we protect ourselves from such instability, guard our eyes from such injustice? Shouldn't we position our young marriage in a safe, happy setting, preparing the way for safe, happy children with a golden retriever?* Yesterday an eighteen year old shared of the January birth of her second child, who has four possible baby daddies. *Shouldn't the government solve societal dysfunction?*

Growing up, my closest encounter with racism was being shamed for my freckles in front of a large group of people. I wanted to crawl under the earth. As an adult, my closest encounter happened Saturday on our porch.

Neighbors Marcus, six, and America, eight, had spent the afternoon in our yard, jumping rope, eating popsicles, and doodling with sidewalk chalk. Somewhere in the midst of the day and in broad daylight, America was sitting on my lap. Her mother noticed this from across the street and deduced that I molested children. About 10 p.m. that night, she sent her enraged older brother to pass along this accusation. "Should she ever see her children on our property again, she will call the police immediately."

I cried much of that night, then again in the alleyway the next morning, receiving a text from another neighbor (and friend of my accuser) while taking out the trash: "R u a jesus follower, or a child follower?" Being accused is awful. Being falsely accused is devastating. I was a mix of tears and anger, shame and confusion. "Maybe I should move to Ontario. Maybe I should never hug or hold a child again. Maybe I was wrong to care for neighborhood children. Maybe there really is something wrong with me?"

It's perplexing to me how Jesus endured false accusation from every angle, and still forgave—still lent hope and hospitality to a legitimately accused thief hanging next to him on the cross. I don't want this posture right now; I want to bite back and curse those who are cursing me.

It feels like ninety percent of our attempts to forgive offenses seem to steer right back into repeat ones. Ninety percent of our perceived notions of imparted grace seem to eventually slap grace in the face and go back to jail. Ninety percent of our prayers seem to go unanswered, or worse, answered antithetically to our plea. And a whopping estimation of about 10 percent pencil in a redemptive story, where from our feeble perceptions, at least, there's a positive outcome. Part of me wants to wallow in this, to throw in the towel and work instead with a high-achieving, healthy crowd who come with a perfect background and smile when they drop a hammer on their foot because life is a gift and they're so grateful to be alive. Part of me wants to work with sinless people, I guess.

When I think about Jesus's time on earth, God himself here among us, I'm baffled by his success rate, or lack thereof. Why did he leave towns to go be alone when people needed him? Why didn't he build a timeless orphanage or hospital to eradicate poverty and disease? Why did he only live thirty-three years, and spend most of these years as a carpenter, cutting, sanding and hammering together pieces of wood? Why did he die, after only a few years of ministry, with so much lingering sorrow, sickness, and injustice? Why did his closest friends often not understand what he was talking about—was his communication that shoddy? Why didn't everyone follow him—weren't his sermons compelling enough, or his miracles outlandish enough, or his story radical enough to capture everyone else's? Apparently not.

Jesus worked really hard and prayed really hard and imparted grace and forgiveness and freedom as heavily and perfectly as any human being ever could, can, or will. And when he left for good, a whole lot of people were left diseased, in jail, paralyzed, unhealed, uninterested in following, enslaved in self, sex, power, money, and drug addiction. Lovely, the Savior of the universe turns up maybe a 10 percent saving rate. Not the happy-clappy message most Sunday pulpits unveil, eh?

I don't think we grasp how deeply the wells of sin delight, nor how darkly the prison of despair enslaves. I think we don't understand how broken we are. And how broken are our perspectives on freedom and grace, prayer and hope, health and true living. English Reformer, John Bradford, was said to have once walked by a drunken man lying unconscious in the gutter in his own vomit. "There, but for the grace of God, go I,"[79] Bradford said. Me too. Even when touching the raw dermis of his nail marks, I think we grasp but a sliver of Jesus and his far-reaching love for us. Maybe about 10 percent of it.

Some years back, I lived in Paris with a Buddhist woman named Jacqueline, an endocrinologist who specialized in nutrition. And Asoumain, a homeless Muslim man from West Africa who'd struggled to find a job for two years, during which time Jacqueline invited him to sleep on her couch. He wore thick, oversized glasses he'd found in a dumpster and his blue shirt or his white one.

During a meal together, I remember conversing about our faith journeys. Asoumain knew that Jacqueline was a Buddhist and that I was a Christ follower. He was unclear as to our differences though, noting we were both "nice" and seemed to want "peace and happiness in the world." Were

---

79 "Grace," in *A New Dictionary of Quotations on Historical Principles from Ancient and Modern Sources*, ed. H. L. Mencken (Alfred A. Knopf: New York, 1942), 488.

not all religions the same, he queried?

"Non," we said, with gentle grins, slowly embarking upon various commonalities, but also undeniable divorces. Jacqueline and I empathized with his struggle, but also knew we shared stark differences. And yet, it was a formative season for me, realizing whether Buddhist, homeless, Christian, or Muslim, in the image of God each has been made. Each bears great dignity, worth, and expression of the Godhead.

The watercolor "La Tour Eiffel" looks at me from across the room. As do flowers on the desk beneath, given by a Muslim friend who came for a cup of coffee. It's been a month since the latest evil tragedy in Paris. Our friend shared of her restrictive upbringing and how from birth, "*hijab* would be her wardrobe, and Allah her god." She shared of being arrested twice by the morality police on account of her scarf being too loose. Then of attending a church in Malaysia where the pastor was murdered—martyred—on her behalf, due to offering a Muslim kindness and hospitality. She shared of newfound curiosities about the Christian God and his tremendous allure, being one who loves not just corporately, but specifically and individually. *Maybe even her,* she's starting to fathom.

"I never heard such an idea. Allah doesn't love. Muslim people don't know they are loved. In Islam, the more you are sad and suffering, the more you are serving Allah. Never does sadness and suffering translate to love though, or joy; it just equals fear." "But I say to you, Love your enemies and pray for those who persecute you,"[80] Jesus says. It's hard to pray for our enemies, and maybe harder to believe the image of God is in them. In every member of ISIS, that is, there is unique image of the Godhead.

Glancing across the street, two children I love pile into their backseat,

---

80 Matthew 5:44.

illegally carrying siblings on their laps. I start remembering the stories—the drunk people and the prostitutes, the addiction and false accusation. Safety is a state of the heart, I remember, and God the true justifier. I remember Jesus' kindness toward children, how he wept and wondered, leaning in at times and knowing to step away at others. I remember that "all we like sheep have gone astray; we have turned—every one—to his own way; and the LORD has laid on him the iniquity of us all."[81] I remember that *I am like my neighbors,* and until I can look the drunkard and prostitute in the eye and say, "Jesus loves you just as much as he does me and apart from the cross of Jesus, I am just as distant from God as you are, and yet with it, just as near; we are equal in our desperation to be forgiven, and equally forgiven by way of His grace"—until I can say that, I think I've yet to grasp the true Gospel.

Sometimes I wonder why God allows us live in his neighborhood.

Five neighbors are coming for drinks and appetizers tonight, Father.
Five neighbors who aren't into you.
Five neighbors made in the image of you.
Five neighbors not made in my image of you.
Would you humble me enough to learn of you through the presence of these friends?

---

81 Isaiah 53:6.

8. LIE

To be alive is to be broken; to be broken is to stand in need of grace.

—*Brennan Manning, The Ragamuffin Gospel* [82]

I called to the Lord from my narrow prison and He answered me in the freedom of space.

—*Victor E. Frankl, Man's Search for Meaning* [83]

---

82 Brennan Manning, *The Ragamuffin Gospel* (Sisters, OR: Multnomah Publishers, 2000), 86.
83 Victor E. Frankl, *Man's Search for Meaning* (Boston, Massachusetts: Beacon Press, 2006), 89.

Road trips growing up meant Pez candy and sneaking into hotel pools. "We aren't hurting anyone, and a quick dip will push us through the afternoon," my parents said. In our family, white lies were advantageous even, "as long they don't hurt anyone."

I took this literally when in my senior year of college we had to make a final group presentation. I may've had to speak for four minutes, tops. That was four minutes too much for my petrified-of-public-speaking self, though; I bailed and said my grandmother died in Florida and I needed to leave town. The professor expressed sincere condolences and allowed me to write my final presentation instead. Lying won again and didn't hurt anyone.

The first time I lied to Micah was about the plaid blue coat. We were new to dating and I was new to weather that required an outside layer.

"Oh this… it's been in my closet forever. Got it at a thrift store back in high school or something."

Twenty minutes later, I caved. Interrupting our random discussion of why glue doesn't stick together in the bottle, I told him I didn't actually buy my coat at the thrift store. Or in high school. I spent forty shiny, brand new dollars on it at Macy's two days before.

In retrospect, I guess I wanted to sound frugal, thoughtful. Like if we ever got married I wouldn't be "one of *those* women," but one who bought groceries with red stickers and spent her money on things that matter, like stamps and supporting my Compassion child in Tanzania. Not a blue plaid coat. For the sake of presenting a likable persona, I was willing to embellish part of my truth—to exaggerate, offer a little white lie, overplay some area to underplay another. Call it what you want, but I lied. And I've decided life is more exciting when I do so.

I gain worth in people's eyes. I seem interesting and worth knowing.

I gain admiration for presenting a life that's not boring.

I gain ground by trumping another's story, surpassing them in my head, if not verbally.

I gain significance in the eyes of man, causing people to like me.

I gain confidence by telling half-truths, or causing laughter by way of sarcasm.

I gain security by fitting in.

I gain safety by covering parts of me that feel insignificant.

I gain control by making people perceive me as in control.

I gain a more captive audience, enhancing one's listening experience and offering a better story.

By lying, it feels like I can provide people with a story worth listening to, albeit a lie.

The fabric on the couch was scratchy the first time I decided not to lie anymore about my dirty little secret. Shame had hidden it for me since I was six. I was shaking and nauseous and felt like there was a good chance the counselor would throw me out of his office to the tone of, "You're a disgusting pervert!" Surely I was a sex addict, I thought, or something deeply removed from a normal human being.

My seven-year-old cousin and I kissed and touched each other in the first room on the right atop the shag carpet staircase. It smelled like moth balls and the paneling was speckled brown. Night was quiet; I could hear my breath and pounding heart, loud, like when you go underwater. He lifted my tie-die tee shirt and touched my chest. It tickled and felt good. The whole scene was like playing house, haphazardly finding ourselves in a locked room where we weren't supposed to be. But I wanted to stay and explore.

Later that summer at a family reunion, I wondered if we could explore again. I remember the bizarre feeling of power as a little girl, able to entice a little boy, to something beyond me, but also very much a part of me. I liked the funny feeling of electricity in my body. And gentle sensation of my lips touching another's. That same reunion weekend, perched under a bed while playing hide-and-seek, my uncle came into the room to undress. Petrified of being caught, I locked my mouth. All I saw were his bare calves and khaki pants hitting the talkative hardwood; the experience paralyzed me. A word was never spoken about any of this, not to my cousin, my uncle, or any diary page. The truth was too risky.

Two decades later, I told the counselor with trepidation. He listened tenderly, normalizing what I shared as a healthy part of maturation. "It would be more weird," he explained, "for a child not to have similar sorts of sexual memories, or fantasies, or curiosities. Sadly though, the majority of the time they get buried deep in sheets of shame for one reason or another."

I remember reading the update from Baby Center nine weeks into pregnancy: "Your baby's external sex organs have arrived." Then at 13: "If you're having a girl, she now has more than two million eggs in her ovaries." TWO MILLION! "What's wrong with me to produce such a horny little newborn?" Essentially I was shocked to remember that sexuality starts at the beginning, unbeknownst to us and thoughtfully known to God. But the shadow of shame positions itself to rarely be far behind.

In the beginning, "man and his wife were both naked and were not ashamed."[84] Seven sentences later, shame seduced, wreaking palpable havoc on every iota of their beings and bodies and homeland. "The eyes of both were opened, and they knew they were naked. And they sewed fig leaves together and made themselves loincloths."[85]

Shame tells me a lullaby of staying in these fig leaves, staying hidden. Shame tells me the vulnerable way will only breed hurt and that he'll help me find places to hide—even hide me when I'm too worn myself. But I've tried these paths and they don't work. They lead me into hiding for days and years and decades. They choke me enough to sustain life, but life as a lie, not life lived alive.

Sexuality is part of us and part of the story Christ is revealing and redeeming over our days. Its promise to keep us hidden will likely come true, but it will also rob liberation. Sexuality is a significant, God-given part of our human makeup. Explorations of what it means to be male, and to be female, both made in the image of God, are a healthy part of growing up and growing into our complex temples.[86] As is embracing that we are sexual beings, not just when pimples and pubic hairs freakishly begin popping out or our first sensation of arousal hits, but from conception.

---

84 Genesis 2:25.
85 Genesis 3:7.
86 See I Corinthians 6:19–20.

Jesus, the Savior we proclaim, was a human being and thus a sexual being, stewarding a sexuality throughout his toddler, child, adolescent and adult years, *just like us.* One of his friends explained our invitation like this: "Little children, abide in him, so that when he appears we may have confidence and not shrink from him in shame at his coming."[87] A modern read sounds something like, "And now, children, stay with Christ. Live deeply in Christ. Then we'll be ready for him when he appears, ready to receive him with open arms, with no cause for red-faced guilt or lame excuses when he arrives."[88]

Your story will be different from mine; maybe you feel obsessively sexual, or obsessively curious about sexual things, or about lying, or cheating, or stealing, or coveting, or killing the FedEx man in your head because he lost your package. Maybe you battle shame for *not* feeling sexual. Maybe you're carrying a memory of sexual abuse, or pornography, or rape, or masturbation, or relations with your same gender. Regardless, what feels dark to you is not dark to God. Before a word is on your tongue, he knows it.[89] You have permission to let it go.

This process of letting go of that for which I am faulted and that which is another's, or that which involves both, rarely happens quickly, let alone easily. I've found it to be a process of forgiveness toward myself and toward those involved. I've also found it to be a process of repentance, an ongoing practice of turning and returning to God, whereby His kindness reorients me back to my safe, forgiven, and true identity.[90] I'm bridged upwards, not downwards, acknowledging my waywardness as couched within the way of Christ's righteousness. My transgressions, that is, shepherd me not toward condemnation, but toward a vision of God's beauty.

---

87 I John 2:28.
88 I John 2:28 (MSG).
89 See Psalm 139:12 and 4.
90 See Romans 2:4.

Day to day, this involves practicing looking at God, maybe visualizing myself in his lap, and the given sin or situation in my hands. Sometimes I feel immediate grief or remorse; other times I must wait on the Spirit to grace such doorways. I consider the cross, pondering Calvary, and that no sin can overturn what Jesus did for me. In this same posture, which may last two minutes, or twenty, I seek to meditate on "the vision of God's beauty," the coming of a restored Eden, the hope of heaven. "Repent, for the kingdom of heaven is at hand,"[91] John the Baptist tells us. Over minutes and months and years, this meditation becomes a reminder that God's kind purposes are often worked out through what once appeared an ugly defeat. It becomes a reminder of Paul's advice, "Beloved, never avenge yourselves, but leave it to the wrath of God,"[92] trusting that he will judge injustice, and I don't have to; nor must I carry it, or compose an auxiliary crucifixion. "Jesus paid it all. It is finished. There is now no condemnation." These doorways of forgiveness and repentance eventually become a pathway back to my true self, and toward the true self I am becoming: Abbie, God's beloved daughter.

Sometimes I also practice letting God look at me. On days when I feel pretty and skinny and steady and patient and secure, I'm the little girl, twirling around the living room to the sparkle of my daddy's adoring gaze. But many days I don't like it. Many days I'm embarrassed for him to look into my eyes. Or see the naked body I cursed while getting dressed this morning. Many days I'm afraid he might see my soul. Though in order to find God in my present, I'm learning, holy in my hardship, I must be willing to face it, to risk being seen in the true state of my heart, and believe he sees it, and still cherishes me.

Non-churchy folks usually say they're non-churchy folks because they

---

91 Matthew 3:2.
92 Romans 12:19.

think churchy folks are hypocritical. I think they've got a point. We're all hypocrites in our own way, the doctors who smoke and use Q-tips, and the devious parts of us that lie and steal and curse in heavy traffic (or are prideful because we don't). Until I face the idolatrous, Judas streams within me, I cannot properly see Christ in me.

Part of humility and a healthy understanding of our humanity seems to mean standing in the tension with the apostle Paul: "I do not understand my own actions, for I do not do what I want, but I do the very thing I hate."[93] We have weaknesses and we have strengths; we lie and we tell the truth; we have bruised parts of our pasts and we have memorable ones. But no part defines us, and all parts contribute to our whole.

In the end, either my lies are uncovered, or I die having never been me. In the end, me is actually the best gift I can offer, the best story I have to tell. For me is made in the image of God, as a child of God, as part of God's Story, told through eternity. And therefore, me as God's daughter—God as my Father, is, in fact, the only story worth telling.

Abba, will you help me tell the truth today? Oh God, who sees us,[94] who knows us more than we know ourselves, would you gaze with healing affection upon our wounds?

---

93 Romans 7:15.
94 See Genesis 16:13.

9. REST

Are you tired? Worn out? Burned out on religion? Come to me. Get away with me and you'll recover your life. I'll show you how to take a real rest. Walk with me and work with me—watch how I do it. Learn the unforced rhythms of grace. I won't lay anything heavy or ill-fitting on you. Keep company with me and you'll learn to live freely and lightly.

—Matthew 11:29–30 (MSG)

Fish tacos turned serious on our date last Friday.

"What's been hard for you about marriage lately?" he asked casually.

Sensations of "oh crap" crawled up my chest. Answering wasn't the scary part. Knowing I'd do well to return the question at some point was. When we got to that inevitable point, he shared that my heart had seemed hard.

"Like in general, or just toward you?"

"Honestly, I think in general. You've seemed hard. Less yourself."

My breath begged for a bigger lung size. My heart also breathed something of a sigh of relief. On the one hand, *I didn't want to know.* On the other, it was as though every part of me had been waiting to know.

Hard-hearted though... *really?* Hitler's daughter may've had that association, but me, sweet and even-keeled me? I never yell (out loud) and am usually cordial to dogs and strangers. Something in me still knew he was right.

"How does your heart feel toward God?" he asked.

"Um... diligent, maybe... and I guess a bit bound?"

I knew "diligence" shouldn't top the goal sheet when shooting for intimacy. As we talked further, the thrust of my hardness traced back to early January, when I'd made a resolution to read through the Bible. Six months in, I was halfway through and with half the heart I started with. "You search the Scriptures because you think that in them you have eternal life; and it is they that bear witness about me, yet you refuse to come to me that you may have life."[95] As my Pharisee genes tend to do, intentions for deeper knowledge caged themselves into a dutiful check-list of performance and pride, perfection and false security. Diligent though I'd been, self-inflicted requirements to read a set portion of Scripture each day had grown me callous.

A.W. Tozer wrote that too many of us have "substituted theological ideas for an arresting encounter; we are full of religious notions but our great weakness is that for our hearts there is no one there... Knowledge by acquaintance," he says, "is always better than mere knowledge by description."[96] I suppose there is the god I want; and there is "the God who is."[97] And often they aren't comrades. At some level, I long for the God who is, but at another (often more persuasive level) I'm perfectly content with the god I want.

The prophet Micah whispered to my weary, diligent soul.

He has told you, O man, what is good;

and what does the LORD require of you

but to do justice, and to love kindness

and to walk humbly with your God? [98]

God apparently doesn't expect of me what I expect of myself. His resolves are simpler, less wrapped in self, less consumed in fixing self. In a few short phrases, he voices resolutions he's into: justice, kindness, humility (i.e., proactivity and being fair, intentionality and being thoughtful,

95 John 5:39-40.
96 A.W. Tozer, *The Divine Conquest* (Old Tappan, N.J.: Fleming H. Revell, 1950), 26, 67.
97 See Exodus 3:14.
98 Micah 6:8.

moving toward him and being nice). And he's told me what he's not into: injustice, unkindness, pride (i.e., silence toward unfairness, apathy toward unkindness, moving away from him and being a jerk).

Lord, I want to want your resolutions in January and in July. I want to want justice and kindness and humility. I want to not want injustice and unkindness and arrogance. I want to abhor unfairness, and unfair things happening around me. In my thoughts and in my actions, I want to learn to be kind. I want to move toward you and I don't want to be an ass. But rituals run deep. My wants and perspectives are not naturally yours. Your requirements are not naturally mine. They are simple, yet impossible, narrowing, yet nothing apart from your Spirit.[99] I need you. To keep defining for me what is good. To keep telling me what is required. To keep redefining my resolutions and resolves toward love.

On a different note, I've felt crampy and bloated for awhile, so took a random pregnancy test this morning. How did this happen? Oh but we longed for this to happen. Unlike the first time around, I already feel a deep sense of closeness, familiarity, even, with the wealth of life wrapped in this growing embryo. I already know it's a son. Granted, we 'knew' Elliana was a son, also; and then she wasn't. I'm elated and enamored and already grieving what was. *Elliana is still a baby—will she forever feel like our first? Lord Jesus, can another human maneuver his or her way into our familiar mix?*

....

Micah: How's your day been?

Me: Bad.

---

99 See John 15:5.

Micah: What's bad?

Me: The motherhood thing.

Micah: Yeah?

Me: Yeah. I don't think I can do it.

Micah: Do you think you can do it today?

Me: I don't know.

Micah: Well, let's just start there.

Me: Okay.

Daddy, please give me this day my daily bread.

This season of erupting interruptions all day long is forcing me to reprioritize and recognize false priorities—to embrace my thoughtfully designed, God-given limits. It's been brutal, but even the stubborn molds of me are starting to think it really may be the truth that sets us free.[100] Among other things, it's forced me to map rhythms, like gratitude and submission and Sabbath, into my story.

I've been practicing this verse from I Thessalonians: "Rejoice always, pray without ceasing, give thanks in all circumstances; for this is the will of God in Christ Jesus for you."[101] Like when I saw *her* and became instantly resentful over her stunning face and pencil thin thighs—*thank you for*

---

100 See John 8:32.
101 I Thessalonians 5:16-18.

84

knitting together this sister so thoughtfully, God and using her in the ways that you are for the Kingdom. Or when I cursed my back fat in the mirror—*thank you for knitting me so thoughtfully.* When folding the third load of laundry, or pairing oodles of socks—*what a gift that my child has legs to walk and run. Thank you for keeping her chilled feet warm, Father. Please comfort those with weary feet today.* When the garbage bill came and we were fined for our neighbor's excess—*forgive me my trespasses as I learn to forgive those trespass against me...*and so on. I can honestly say giving thanks for people and things, particularly those I don't like, has lessened the sting a bit. Maybe practicing gratitude captures lies, "takes captive every thought to make it obedient to Christ,"[102] no longer accentuating faults, but our gracious Trinity who forgives faults. But I still have a long way to go, learning gratitude and learning submission.

Micah made me a delicious chai latte this morning. I tried to storm out the door as he tried to hand it to me, passive aggressively communicating that I was too consumed with buttoning buttons and divvying out teething tablets to enjoy the luxury of his frothy concoction. In retrospect, he was trying to serve me and enjoy some sips of tea before heading into our respective Mondays; I was trying to say I wanted help with that 6 a.m. diaper, or 7 a.m. chin that was covered in snot. I was trying to voice my desperation surrounding this new role as a mom that I can't quite find a rhythm to. Instead I projected all sorts of frustrated shenanigans and ended up in tears.

This parenting thing has brought up ranges of emotions in both of us, from madly in love, to massively surreal and overwhelmed sensations surrounding the responsibilities involved. Micah has felt new layers of financial fear, as well as jealousy at times toward affections I feel with Elliana, almost as if he's been pushed aside. It's also tapped into longings

---

102 See II Corinthians 10:5.

with his own mom, wishing they shared a deeper emotional bond. For nine plus months, a baby was predominantly attaching to me. He expected that when she was born, he could carry half the load and share an obvious and immediate connection too. We're both learning our engagements are unique though, and 100 percent in their own way. We're also learning that two nursing boobs makes a tremendous difference in who a baby prefers the lap of. Soon enough, I don't doubt Micah will be connecting more naturally pushing her up the driveway on a bike, or explaining how to hammer a nail, but right now my connection feels more natural. And that's felt rightfully hard and sad at times.

I'm finding it goes a long way to express to him small points of gratitude, reminding him of the crucial role he plays in our family, as a husband and as a father. The times he unloads the dishwasher, or turns on the noise machine, makes the bed, or pays the Georgia Power bill—his willingness to get up every morning to go work and provide for our family—these seemingly ordinary tasks I now see as meaningful forms of grace, and it's helped to tell him so.

So easily I forget that Micah is tired and learning too, and at times frustrated with our new and blurry normals. I also forget that he can't read my mind. And that by sharing pieces of my inner world, submitting myself to his love, he is better able to understand and lead us out.

Out of respect for Christ, be courteously reverent to one another. Wives, understand and support your husbands in ways that show your support for Christ. The husband provides leadership to his wife the way Christ does to his church, not by domineering but by cherishing. So just as the church submits to Christ as he exercises such leadership, wives should likewise submit to their husbands. Husbands, go all out in your love for your wives, exactly as Christ did for the church—a love marked by giving, not getting. Christ's love makes the church whole. His words evoke her beauty. Everything he does and says is designed to bring the best out of her, dressing her in dazzling white silk, radiant with holiness.

—Ephesians 5:21–27 (MSG)

Women, he seems to say, your submission should express itself to Christ and to your husband. Husbands, your submission should imitate the endless love Christ has for his bride, the Church, embodying tremendous expressions of protection, nourishment, and cherishing. Apparently when we let submission translate into its intended meanings, beginning with love, it lets us relax into something good—someone who's trustworthy. Submission starting at Christ's submission on our behalf[103] is of the highest invitations. Not unlike the discipline of Sabbath maybe.

Through most of my twenties, "Sabbath" wasn't part of my weekly rhythm. In my mind it meant either napping all day, or a vigilant Judaic approach that refused work altogether. And neither fit my paradigm, or seemed half appealing, so I carried on with my busy (often ministry related) pace, acting as if God never mentioned rest. Turns out the English Standard Version of the Bible references "rest" 521 times, and "Sabbath" 150.

After a three-week solitude retreat in Washington State, opening my eyes to reasons I resist the Sabbath, plus marrying someone who had a balanced, inviting view, I decided to enter the gates of weekly rest. Here's what I've concluded: For me, skipping the Sabbath is either a trust issue or a pride one. Either I don't believe God can keep the world on its axis if I take a day off, or I'd rather be in control of my Sunday than spend it resting with him.

---

103 See I Peter 2:24 and 3:18.

God rested after the work of creation, implying that I have permission to (and was actually commanded to, probably in part because the permission piece wouldn't sell.) Even as a nursing mom, loaded down in breast milk and obligatory details required to keep my child alive, I've found there are ways to be lavished in God's rest. There are ways to be mindfully gracious on ourselves (and I daresay obedient) one seventh of the week. *"Let us therefore strive to enter that rest,"* the writer of Hebrews exhorts,[104] from the work that is wearing for us, that is, whether bills, laundry, dishes, or grocery shopping, God tells us to give ourselves a break, trusting they'll kindly wait until Monday morning. Community may play into this, as well as generous husbands, and no doubt it will look different for a chunk of years while infants and children are dependent on us. But at any stage, really, it's a discipline that will require seasonal tweaking and grace, and probably won't ever fit squarely into a box.

To see and remember seems something of a spiritual responsibility. Carving out times to feast and to fast, to ponder and confess, to celebrate and to grieve—these seem crucial to our staying alive as Christ followers. "Pressing pause," acknowledging that, "Yes, God, you were in our midst this week. You are good and faithful and we remember your story through all weeks of history. We can lay down our defenses and rest because of what you've done."

"The Sabbath was always a hallmark of the Jews throughout their history," says author Peter Scazzero. "This one act, perhaps more than any other, kept them from the pressure of the powerful cultures that have sought to assimilate them. For this reason it is often said that for thirty-five hundred years, the Sabbath has kept the Jews more than Jews have kept the Sabbath."[105] The word Sabbath comes from *Shabbat*, which literally

104 Hebrews 4:11.
105 Peter Scazzero, *Emotionally Healthy Spirituality* (Nashville, TN: Thomas Nelson, 2011), 165.

means to stop.[106] For Micah and me, the main goal of a Sabbath, whether on a Sunday or Tuesday, is to cease from our usual rhythms of work. This typically looks something like worshipping with our quirky little family of Anglican saints and then pursuing portions of rest throughout the remainder of the day. Sometimes that means returning for an evening service. Always it means lingering more than usual. Often I'll ask Micah to be on child duty and allow me some solitude (every couple months I try to do a longer version of this, for a full day or weekend). Depending on what his week looked like, he may appreciate the same. For Micah, roasting coffee is restful, as is practicing Lectio Divina, or browsing an architecture magazine. For me, maybe it's a bubble bath, journaling, or baking a batch of cookies. We nap if possible and leave space for spontaneity and play. We may share a meal with friends, paint, or walk in the woods. Sometimes we try fixed hour prayer together,[107] dance in our living room, or picnic in a park. The bottom line is, we intentionally strive to enter God's rest for a day.[108]

106 *Wikipedia, the Free Encyclopedia*, s.v. "Shabbat," accessed June 9, 2017, https://en.wikipedia.org/wiki/Shabbat/.
107 Phyllis Tickle, "About Fixed-Hour Prayer," *The Works of Phyllis Tickle*, accessed June 9, 2017, http://www.phyllistickle.com/fixed-hour-prayer/.
108 See Hebrews 4:11.

10. MANNA

Love is patient and kind; love does not envy or boast; it is not arrogant or rude. It does not insist on its own way; it is not irritable or resentful; it does not rejoice at wrongdoing, but rejoices with the truth. Love bears all things, believes all things, hopes all things, endures all things.

—I Corinthians 13:4—7

Me at dinner: Thank you for making all this. Sorry I got distracted online and didn't help.

Him: It's okay; you did all that cleaning.

Me: Yeah, but you gave Elliana a bath.

Him: How about we don't keep accounts, light a candle, and eat.

The day is done and I write from hands and knees on a medicine ball, the most "comfortable" position at this point of pregnancy. My friend Jesse, a physician assistant, reminded me babies in utero are like parasites, sucking feverishly from my energies and wellness. Yes, I concur. It's been a rough chunk of months growing this life. Few days have passed without toil. Elliana is a mere fifteen months. Were we thinking straight nine-ish months back?

It feels like two of us had sex, and now one of us is bearing the responsibility, and being affected at every level of every cell of her body for every day of the rest of her life by the ensuing fruit. It doesn't feel fair. Maybe sexual differences are like appetite. Some of us feel satisfied, or full even, the grand majority of the time, and the thought of more isn't appealing. Some of us are like the athletic teen in puberty who has a gallon of milk plus two double cheese whoppers and still has capacity for more, day or night. No judgment, but I digress.

When I was single we dated more, God and me. We went to coffee shops and read for hours on end. Sat on the couch. Went hiking and picnicked in wide fields. We knelt together in my closet where no one else could hear. I miss that. I miss him. Started dating another. Then got engaged. A hurdle grew between my maker and me. Getting married grew it higher. Requested more intentionality. Required sharing intimacy.

I knew I had to let go of something, lest I die. I scheduled times to sneak away with him. Prioritized his intimacy over the altar where I said "I do." Then a baby came, and now there's another. The hurdle seems impossible. Interruptions have become my holy rhythm, and dreamed-of roles my daily feast, but far from my manna.

I am full and I am hungry. I miss him, the one who pursued me first.[109] Before my second him, and tiny her and him. Cheating seems my only option, lest I die. And I've been dying lately. Pulling away has gotten harder. Less time and space and undivided attention. Less intimacy.

Truly, truly, I say to you, unless a grain of wheat falls into the earth and dies, it remains alone; but if it dies, it bears much fruit.

—John 12:24

Timothy Keller says, "We never imagine that getting our heart's deepest desires might be the worst thing that can ever happen to us."[110] In subtle ways, that resonates. For decades my heart desired being a mother, as well as being wife (probably in that order). But committing to it exclusively, abiding in it faithfully, has led me down a naked aisle. Has left me feeling somehow lonely, and less in touch than I used to be with God.

Some part of me believed a husband would fix things, albeit friends told me otherwise. Lightbulbs do get changed more often, and I do get to share a bed with my best friend. But my complexities and peculiarities and insecurities are by and large the same. I thought having a man tell

---

109 See I John 4:19.
110 Timothy Keller, *Counterfeit Gods: The Empty Promises of Money, Sex, and Power, and the Only Hope That Matters* (UK: Penguin Books, 2011), 1.

me I was pretty every day would make me feel pretty every day. Even when feeling chunky or with my drawers down. Some days it does—the mirror and I do okay, and I'm able to celebrate my body and other girls' bodies and beauty. Others days it doesn't. I thought it would fix my social anxiety. Some level of me thought it would fix my anxiety altogether. I thought it would fix my loneliness.

As a single person I thought, "At least if I married, I could face this despair with someone." Now there are moments when I think, "At least then I could do it myself and my opinion was always the right one." I thought having a husband and sex and a house and a dog would make me content. I still think up scenarios that should surely secure my contentment— traveling to Vietnam, a boisterous Thanksgiving table with two biological and two adopted children, a sizzling turkey, and a husband who gently leans to kiss my cheek and say he loves me.

Am I that naïve, or stubborn, to not remember that things or people or ideals won't satisfy—weren't made to satisfy? Yes. I forget that "ideal" isn't real, and I'm prone to keep wandering toward just that. I forget God. I forget that I'm human, and in continual need of renovation.

Frustrated by puff and sag and dullness in the rearview mirror today, it dawned on me that no matter how lovely my visage, or how often Micah affirms my worth, if I'm not affirmed in divine worth, I'm stuck in a dead-end lie. No matter how wonderful marriage, or orgasms, the number on the scale, or the number in our bank account, these things won't fix me, or offer lasting significance.

"I love you with a love that will fail you," he'll often say upon leaving. We try to remind each other that each other will never be enough. That he can give me everything, but that won't cut it. That I can be the most astounding wife and mom and homemaker and miss life—miss my true calling. I can gain the world, and all its capacities for knowledge, nurture, insight, intellect, health, balance, fortitude, strength, and admiration, and still lose my soul.

I was a freshman in college when I started caring about God. Not long after, I started caring about the things and thoughts of God. Intervarsity Christian Fellowship was the campus ministry that ushered my initial engagements with Jesus. I remember it like yesterday when the staff worker, Kim, was speaking at our weekly gathering; she began by telling stories about joys of marriage with her husband Jeff. Then she took a sharp turn, launching into a theme that shattered a part of me that's never been the same.

Kim explained how Jeff didn't complete or fully satisfy her, nor provide her with a secure identity. And she said he never would. No matter how much he loved, honored, and cherished her, Kim said out loud that Jeff would never be enough to quench her longings. I hated these words. I thought they were exaggerated and coarse. Previously I'd held a deep admiration for this couple, considering their marriage attractive and enchanting. Now it seemed unromantic and hollow. Little did I know, however, that what Kim shared that evening would be a gift to my marriage many years later, as well as to my relationship with God.

Friends came for lunch Sunday. They've been engaged a month, set to marry in March and must be the most mature twenty-two and twenty-three year olds you've ever met. But as I stared across our table of champagne cupcakes at the almost newlyweds, I remembered Kim's words. And I remembered my few years of marriage. She was right: he will never be enough for her, and she will never be enough for him.

My husband is more of a romantic than me, but no matter how deep, or high, or wide, or mighty a lover's love, it will never be enough. It will never quench our soul's depths, or capture the heavenly heights for which we were made. No longer is that troubling news though. In fact, it's been liberating, slowly reordering my attachments and lifting pressure off my husband and babies and mom and mother-in-law and friends—all of whom will inevitably let me down at some point, possibly this afternoon.

Our now is a shadow of what's to come, I'm learning. Micah's and my journey as a married two is but a temporary companionship ushering us toward One. We were made to be captured by the rest of Christ, found by the altar of God's marriage. "For God alone, O my soul, wait in silence," David prayed in Psalm 62, "for my hope is from him. He only is my rock and my salvation, my fortress; I shall not be shaken. On God rests my salvation and my glory; my mighty rock, my refuge is God. Trust in him at all times, O people; pour out your heart before him; God is a refuge for us" (5–8).

Lord, will you help me choose you today? Cherish you at the cost of cheating another? Cheating another to abide in you?

....

Water dove through my fingers as I rinsed the hot pink raspberries. I winced as the darling inside of me felt like it was doing the same, winsomely diving through moments and milestones, collapsing into new forms faster than I can document.

Tomorrow marks twenty-seven weeks. I sobbed at breakfast, unsure whether I can make it to the end. Pelvic pain, aggressive kicks, reflux, swelling—standing hurts, but so does lying down. I resonate somehow with Jesus' plea: *"Father, if you are willing, remove this cup from me. Nevertheless, not my will, but yours, be done."*[111] Weary though I am, part of me wishes life had a pause button these days, too, a way to contain the plethora of blurs so synonymous with how I envision heaven. Elliana reached for our hands at that same breakfast table and for the first time and exclaimed, "pay, pay, pay," so we bowed our heads before maple syrup and raspberry French toast, and "payed." Literal warmth bellowed from within, seemingly beyond my capacity to bear.

From there we made our way to the hospital, swinging to yet a new polarity of emotion. Rosary beads rested on Grampy's table; death knelt near. Ninety-two years have bid him well and worn him weak. We're all dying in some sense, but his skeletal, pneumonia-laden self with a loud "DNR" bracelet seemed closer to death than my mid-thirties one.

Micah and I took him to five o'clock mass a few weeks ago. Punctual as always, he waited by the bench at the assisted living entrance. Per usual greeting, he hobbled into the front passenger's seat, thanked us for taking him, and reiterated, "I wanna leave as soon as the bread and wine part is done. And then give the bulletin to your (unbelieving and doesn't really care about it) Mother." Easy enough. We passed Piggly Wiggly and turned left at the traffic light. I was half listening as Grampy rambled about poisonous food and dropping him off out front so he wasn't late.

"Hey Abb, ever seen one of these?" he said, retrieving a little orange thing, about the size of a dime, from his pocket.

"Dried mango maybe?"

---

111 Luke 22:42.

The car started reeking of bad perfume.

"Brought it to my nurse today. Told her maybe it gave me the rash."

"You're allergic to dried fruit?"

"It's not dried fruit; it's for the air."

"For the air?"

"Yeah, freshens the air. The nurse told me old people smell bad and ladies like it."

"Grampy, you ate potpourri?"

"I don't know, Abb," he raised his voice, "I ate whatever this damn little orange thing is, which apparently isn't what you're supposed to do with it."

"Did it taste good?"

"Good enough. Did the trick of covering my breath for mass last week."

"Grampy, you don't smell the rankness in our car right now, from that one little piece?"

"Old people can't smell. It was in a bowl on the table, like peanuts or something. So I ate a handful. Found it in my pocket today, so brought it to show my nurse, thinking maybe it was the culprit for that rash last week."

Micah and I exchanged wide, smiling eyes in the rearview mirror.

"You think that smelly stuff will kill me?"

"Apparently not, Grampy, but it probably was the culprit for your rash."

"Aw, hell," he said, sticking the piece back in his pocket. "Drop me off in the front so I'm not late."

Even unconscious, I could hear Grampy reminding me, "I leave at communion," and, "Give the bulletin to your Mother."

Elliana stuffed sweet potatoes into her mouth at the hospital cafeteria. I envisioned Grampy doing so nearly a century ago. Seasons of life seem too short. I thought about the life in my uterus, hounding me with expectation. I imagined its young breaths, confidently taking shelter in my being, and observed frustrated breaths from Grampy, as if searching for a shelter beyond. To love, maybe, is to lose the safety of not losing, to expose oneself to the ache of absence.

Darling Child,

What are your dreams and expectations for this life? Where does your hope rest? I can't tell you much, but I can tell you that in all its brilliance, life will also give you brokenness, exhaustion, and eventually your physical death. No life escapes it, though a narrow few escape its sting. There will be but one with whom you will find refuge, even in death,[112] *and pleasure beyond measure through all seasons of life. You'll be persuaded otherwise, but I promise that persuasion will never meet your needs or provide the joy you're designed for. To set your hope in this world will leave you in despair, but to cheat the world for the sake of the Spirit, even as your soul takes new form this week, will lead you to true life and peace.*[113]

With deepest affections,

Mommy

---

112 See Proverbs 14:32.
113 See Romans 8:6.

11. DEEPER

Truly, truly, I say to you, you will weep and lament, but the world will rejoice. You will be sorrowful, but your sorrow will turn into joy. When a woman is giving birth, she has sorrow because her hour has come, but when she has delivered the baby, she no longer remembers the anguish, for joy that a human being has been born into the world. So also you have sorrow now, but I will see you again, and your hearts will rejoice, and no one will take your joy from you.

—John 16:20-22

My body felt used the first time. He was as gentle and gracious as one could be, but I still felt used. After being tugged and sucked and torn and tired, I was being asked to give yet again.

Its been six blurry, euphoric, exhausting weeks since our son was born. Parts of my left nipple still throb. All of my soul still throbs, wondering at the magnificent, sacred journey of bearing and delivering life, shattering me into a thousand fragile pieces. *Will I be this fragile forever? Have I been this fragile forever, but somehow able to mask the exposing marks?*

The thin, croissant-like paper crinkled beneath me. In soft tones, the physician assistant examined my tears and inquired about holiday plans. *I was cleared.* And now deeply troubled, being asked to reopen that part of myself that had just endured so much. My understandings of making love moved countless layers deeper.

With Elliana, we didn't find out the gender and went into the birth with various name choices, which was quite a thrilling process. With our second, we did find out and did choose a name beforehand, which has similarly been quite a thrilling process.

Naming a soul, speaking a prayerful expression over one's life, we've found to be a humbling and honorable act. It's made me think about God asking Adam to name the animals. "Now out of the ground the LORD God had formed every beast of the field and every bird of the heavens and *brought them to the man to see what he would call them.* And whatever the man called every living creature, that was its name."[114] Surely God had some names in mind while forming earth's animals, but he brought them to Adam, humbly submitting to his creativity and lead.

---

114 Genesis 2:19 (emphasis mine).

Though it seemed a tad outlandish, I asked God if I could "labor in the Spirit," wanting to be aware somehow that he was *with me* throughout, *walking with me* throughout. I can genuinely say that happened. After an arduous four weeks of pre-laboring, actual labor lasted just four hours, and felt gradual, manageable, attainable, even, like that wicked final incline before the summit. I showed up to the birthing center at seven centimeters. I remember us walking uncomfortably, but expectantly, on trails behind the building, quietly singing "It Is Well with My Soul."

At some point we came inside. Cervix ripened, I crawled onto the sheets, white with mercy, for the final push. Wincing moved into the dark groan as Micah held my right leg. The midwife whispered through the scorching ring, "Do you want to touch his head?" I declined, unable to cradle such hope, whilst still saddled in such despair. Two more pushes and "delight" stared trustingly into my eyes. He took no falling for. I was madly in love; we were madly in love. You shall be called, "Eden."

His name signifies relationship, perfect union with its intricate architect. Its Hebrew root is "delight," inviting rest and communion, a call to abide in the Vine who shall never tire of tending to and pouring into his masculine frame. Eden is a prayer of trajectory, of movement toward the Father, that we might savor the feasts of his table. Eden is "a place of pleasure," a place that was, and is becoming. It lends hope to our present, to a "kingdom" within, and hope to our future, a kingdom being marvelously sculpted.

David Benner says, "Made in God's image, humans are invested with a nonnegotiable dignity. We are compatriots of God, not just creatures of God. Even more astounding, God chooses us to be his friends. That imputed status was never annulled, despite our sinful rebellion and declarations of independence."[115] "Deep down, however," Benner goes on

---

115 David G Benner, *Surrender to Love* (Downers Grove, IL: Intervarsity Press, 2003), 23.

to say, "something within us seems to remember the Garden within which we once existed. Part of us longs to return; we know that this is where we belong. But another part of us seems bent on living out our illusions of freedom and autonomy. We tell ourselves that we can create other gardens in which to find soul rest and encounter love. But what we create are weed-infested gardens of compulsion and idolatry. Instead of rest we get addiction and self-preoccupation."[116]

In the brief span of Genesis 2 and 3 (though Ezekiel and Revelation shine much here too), the Word, who is Christ, tells us the glorious story of paradise gained, and of paradise lost. It tells us about home and home's hijacking, when a curious hand was tantalized by a seemingly satisfying fruit and a voice that said, "God doesn't really love you, does he? Surely His provisions and visions for your life aren't that astounding?" And it points us to a new Eden, a City restored, a Paradise rediscovered. It points us to Jesus, paving the way between cities, lost and found.

Dearest Son,
May you embrace adventure, that your masculinity would lead you deep into meaningful participation with justice and truth, beauty and freedom. May you stay and be made, then someday go and make, endeavoring toward that which draws you to marvel and wonder, leaving you breathless and weak with awe where hidden glory lies, where burning bushes hide. May your life be stirred by affections for the King and his Kingdom, and whether we are allowed to know you for one hour on this earth, or one lifetime, may we speak your name with prayerful expectation, allowing it to remind us of true rest, of perfect union and reunion with the arms of the Papa we were made for, the City for which true life was born.
With Love, Mommy

....

---

116 Ibid, 24.

Earl Grey sits to my left, laptop to my front. Deep breath. And another. Elliana tugs unremittingly at my pant leg to zip her purple princess dress. I zip her purple princess dress. This sleep deprivation feels eerily similar to high-school days, when we snuck into the liquor cabinet, got drunk, did foolish things, and felt like death in the morning. Eden projects a raspy cough in the room beside me, the type of cough that doesn't scare you if it's your cough, but petrifies you when it's your son's, because you're responsible. You're the one who decides if it's bad enough to need medicine, call the pediatrician, or go the ER. These things aren't covered in pre-marital counseling.

Every other Wednesday a crew comes over for dinner and Bible study. Last night a girl joined us for the first time, expressing afterwards the gift of being in a home with caring people. It was a good reminder that people can experience connection with God when God's people love one another.[117] And that hospitality and kindness are rare and powerful, maybe because they're alive and real.

I've been missing these lately, the alive and the real. How can I be pouring my days into two stunningly alive and real little gems, and yet feel so deadened at times? Anxiety feels like a louder companion than Jesus, which I suspect plays into this connection. My soul was packed this afternoon with faces and gossip and interactions and relationships, yet I was alone in our house the entire time. We live in bizarre times with bounties of images—myriads of images. And ideas. And stimulation. And quasi-connections—myriads of quasi-connections and false intimacy. Dizzying amounts of true and false and maybe information.

Last week I turned off my phone and computer. I try to do this seasonally, intentionally creating space—to remember and acknowledge and dream.

---

117 See John 13:35.

It was a meaningful fast, but instead of its usual reviving effect, it revealed deeper depravity. Deeper grief, like a depleted balloon, depressed of air, chopped of capacities and familiarities of what it means to rise. I miss undisturbed space. Undivided direction. Literally as I write this sentence, a darling is beginning to wake. Moving toward the crib, I grieve another train of thought gone.

A handful of summers ago, I'd just finished up my first year in seminary. It had been a long year, and in an entirely different context (mateless and childless) my soul felt similarly crammed and depleted. So I boarded a plane for a remote city in Africa to hold orphaned babies for a few months. These little gems taught me about weakness and reverence, grief and redemption, breathing and true life. "Health," I heard a psychology professor say during that season, is "stewarding a continual state of grief." In other words, stewarding awareness of a broken world in search of redemption.

A friend recently encouraged me to do something "lasting" each day, like painting, or quilting (I'd have to learn how first), or writing a letter. And then the yellow wrapper of my Luna bar this morning read, "Do something for your future self." Minus any theological implication, maybe the messages are the same. Given that mopped floors get sticky again, meals get eaten, and clean diapers will soon be soiled, the idea is to record our days with something of permanence—reminding us we're not just spinning our wheels, but thoughtfully chosen to build into a lasting City[118]—an eternal beauty.

Viktor Frankl explores pieces of this conversation in his evocative work *Man's Search for Meaning*[119]. Based on time spent in five different Holocaust

---

118 See Revelation 21:2.
119 I don't dare make a tight comparison here between motherhood and a concentration camp, but Frankl invites exploration of a broader suffering, to which monotony and an easily

work camps, Frankl exposits theories on suffering, and particularly on the sufferers who eventually survive:

> *The Latin word finis has two meanings: the end or the finish, and a goal to reach. A man who could not see the end of his "provisional existence" was not able to aim at an ultimate goal in life. He ceased living for the future, in contrast to a man in normal life. Therefore the whole structure of his inner life changed; signs of decay set in which we know from other areas of life...*
>
> *A man who let himself decline because he could not see any future goal found himself occupied with retrospective thoughts... But in robbing the present of its reality there lay a certain danger. It became easy to overlook the opportunities to make something positive of camp life, opportunities which really did exist...*[120]

> *A creative life and a life of enjoyment are banned to him. But not only creativeness and enjoyment are meaningful. If there is a meaning in life at all, then there must be meaning in suffering. Suffering is an ineradicable part of life, even as fate and death. Without suffering and death human life cannot be complete.*

> *The way in which a man accepts his fate and all the suffering it entails, the way in which he takes up his cross, gives him ample opportunity—even under the most difficult circumstances—to add deeper meaning to his life.*[121]

At the National Prayer Breakfast in 2013, Kathy Keller based her talk on a book by Paul Billheimer called, *Don't Waste Your Sorrows:* "I was told about it years and years ago, but which I have never read. I've never read it because I was so struck by the title that I've been meditating about it ever since. The thought that I could go through life with its inevitable pain, disappointment, even tragedy and have it yield nothing of value, alter

---

lost sense of purpose in motherhood came to mind.
120 Ibid. 70-72.
121 Ibid., 67-68.

nothing in my character, produce nothing with which to comfort other people, is insupportable. It's unacceptable. If I waste my encounters with suffering and pain by indulging in stoicism or despair, or depression or bitterness, then they will have no meaning for me and will be of no use to you. It would seem like a magnification of the tragedy if I went through terrible times and had nothing to show for it personally, and nothing to offer because of it relationally."[122] Neither do I want to waste my sorrows today. On the one hand, I'm smitten like never before by the role of motherhood, while on the other, I'm missing what once was. Adoring while grieving, beginning while ending, becoming while letting go.

In Bible theory, at least, "children are a gift of the LORD."[123] But there's an easily-swallowable pill passed around translating this as: "raising children should always feel happy and blessed." But maybe children are a gift from the Lord, not because they always make life chipper, but because they're a thoughtful and ongoing means of drawing us nearer to the Lord, of looking more like him?

After some focused minutes down yonder during a diaper change earlier, I glanced at Eden's face. Flushed cheeks, happily round like a lollipop, he was beaming. It was the connection a mother dreams of. And I almost missed it. Because I was consumed with the task of cleaning his other cheeks. Not unimportant, but also not the main point. The main point is always the person. Yet another reminder that I crave connection today. Alive connection, with my self, with my son, with those with whom I cross paths. And true connection always transcends the task.

Sometimes I envision what it might have been like for Adam and Eve

---

122 Kathy Keller, "Don't Waste Your Sorrows," *Westminster Theological Seminary Bookstore*, accessed June 9, 2017, http://www.wtsbooks.com/common/pdf_links/9780525952459-dont-waste-your-sorrows.pdf.
123 Psalm 127:3–5, NASB.

to walk with God.[124] Their stroll feels life-giving, consistently caught off guard by striking features gazing back at them. They seem connected, genuinely interested, and delighted by one another's image. I crave that notice of my Maker, and the striking features of his face. I crave that true connection, as I swipe a soiled bottom, or tarry in my tasks this afternoon. I crave notice of his beaming smile, as I reach for my tea and take another deep breath. Again, my understandings of making love moved countless layers deeper.

LORD, you have been our dwelling place

in all generations.

Before the mountains were brought forth,

or ever you had formed the earth and the world,

from everlasting to everlasting you are God.

The years of our life are seventy,

or even by reason of strength eighty;

yet their span is but toil and trouble;

they are soon gone, and we fly away.

So teach us to number our days

that we may get a heart of wisdom.

Satisfy us in the morning with your steadfast love,

that we may rejoice and be glad all our days.

Let your work be shown to your servants,

---

124 See Genesis 3:8.

and your glorious power to their children.

Let the favor of the Lord our God be upon us,

and establish the work of our hands upon us;

yes, establish the work of our hands!

(Lines from Psalm 90, a prayer of Moses.)

12. GROWTH

Lent
Prepare.
Listen. Sacrifice. Deny.
Endure. Permission.
Darkness. Rest.
Ponder.
Love.
Sin.
Truth. Watch. Receive.
Lies. Led.
Light. Death. Risen.
Freedom.
Obey. Pain. Feast.
Gain. Die.
Jesus.
Risen. Live. Suffering.
Space. Trust. Doubt.
Touch.
Find. Joy. Doubt.
Believe. Confess. Ask. Wait.

Evening, morning and noon I cry out in distress, and he hears my voice.

—Psalm 55:17 (NIV)

Prior to having kids, I judged parents who snapped at their kids. Now I empathize, and beg for the grace to be compassionate and slow to anger. Two kids has taken me to the brink of a boiling point I didn't know was there. It's also convinced me that the non-fruits of the Spirit—the jealousy, the strife, the anger[125]—are mostly nature, not nurture. Had Elliana been in school yet or daycare, I would've blamed those environments. But I'm with her most hours of most days, and in the past week, they've all reared their heads. In her and in me.

My days feel erasable, so I'm writing in pencil. The long awaited letter came. "With sincere respect, your manuscript is not a fit for our publishing house," they told me in black Times New Roman. "Screw your respectful publishing house," my flesh snapped back, spinning in rejection, questioning my worth and worthiness. I didn't know how meaningless my life as a mom felt until opening that envelope; I didn't know that proposal held a convincing assurance that my days mattered. And now they don't. *Maybe I don't.* My pity party can last about thirty minutes and then two little people will wake wanting cheeks wiped and Cheerios poured in a bowl, which feels like something anyone with half a brain could do.

And yet, there they are, deep in a world of dreams through the crack of the door—his fiercely handsome profile and her angelic frame in that white dress, unchanged from the morning service. Elisabeth Elliot once wrote, "The secret is Christ in me, not me in a different set of circumstances."[126] Indeed, these circumstances seem debilitating, Jesus, this rejection numbing. But thank you for that crack in the door; thank you for cracked glimpses into beauty, an assured glimpse into glory. In a

---

125 See Galatians 5:19-21.
126 Debbie MacDaniel, "Forty Inspiring Quotes from Elisabeth Elliott," *CrossWalk,* accessed June 9, 2017, http://www.crosswalk.com/faith/spiritual-life/inspiring-quotes/40-inspiring-quotes-from-elisabeth-elliot.html.

few short minutes, I get to be your hands and feet—God in a body to these babies you've given me, these babies I so fervently want to give back to you—your babies—too young yet to leap spiritually and intellectually into belief. Thank you; what a vast privilege, Christ. What a marked position of honor. Would you help me trust today that it was, in fact, you who thoughtfully deemed that manuscript "unfit" for the time being—and that you've also deemed these darlings to be uniquely mine.

Our friend Bob got released from jail on Monday and has been staying with us. He's manic depressive and intimate with crack. I've learned to love addicts before. I've fallen in love with addicts before. I've learned to love the addict in myself before. But this time has been different.

Suicide would've taken Bob's life years ago, but his childhood Catholicism sings anthems of hell that scare him away. And scare him from God, too. We ate homemade pizza his first night with us; I remember feeling oddly glamorous—sickeningly virtuous, even—because we had an ex-convict in our home.

Bob's company has reminded me that people aren't usually as scary as we think, and there's such a thing as brilliant, creative, kind criminals. He's reminded me that freedom's battlefield is ultimately within, and healing isn't about not *falling*, but learning tools to help us stand back up. That dignity breeds dignity, and healthy transitions require healthy bridges—that we're all criminals at some level, and some of us get caught. Bob's company has also driven me flat crazy.

Spent last night after a long day together, the last thing I wanted to do was think or talk, especially about meaningful things. Micah proceeded to share how God had been unveiling things to him through Bob, like his tendency to hide and grow stale in his willingness to be changed, ignoring Christ for lesser trades of dependence and legalism, perfectionism and blame. His humility was annoying and sexy. And compelled mine.

I'm addicted and intimate with so many things apart from you, dear Jesus. And yet your rope never ends for me. So often I don't seek help, or see the reality that anything's wrong. So often I'm stuck believing lies. Believing there couldn't be a better story. So often I stay stuck in fears. Thank you for healing me, Jesus. How I need you.

....

"Home in 20," his text read.

"k. love you. even tho i burnt the lasagna."

It's been one of those weeks. Eden can't fall asleep. Normally he'd sleep till February if I let him. This evening he's restless, as if aware of a world not right, feeling crammed into a space not intended as home. I held his tears, their authenticity reaching in to mine.

Postpartum depression has rudely interrupted my life. It's been dark and scary and paralyzing, hollow and anxious, all in one breath. I went on medication. My friend Stephanie told me that was brave.

About three months into Eden, I realized it was more than newborn fog. A toothpick could lean the wrong way and I'd end up sad, scared, and anxious. With few commitments, even, my limit felt tapped, always at my edge. Removed and apathetic, I tended robotically to Elliana and Eden's needs, desperate for Micah's return from work. I wasn't tempted to drive off a road, per se, but there were certainly times it wouldn't have been surprised if I did. "Oh, that I had wings like a dove!" my soul empathized with the Psalmist, "I would fly away and be at rest; I would wander far away; I would lodge in the wilderness; *Selah*. I would hurry to find a shelter from the raging wind and tempest."[127] Happy, giggly, intimate moments happened, but only about three percent of the time. When I called my OB, the on-call nurse responded with a sarcastic version of, "What are the symptoms that would make you think you have postpartum?" I started crying and hung-up. The nurse who called back was a gem and applauded me for having the courage to reach out.

Eden rocks in my arms and I cry out to God for reprieve from the depression, and the spinach that's had me down with food poisoning, and the friend who told me today of her crumbling marriage. I think of our friend Carl.

When I first met this neighbor, he could see shadows of shadows, and prayed every morning that diabetes wouldn't rob his vision completely. Today Carl is completely blind. In some ways he accepts this answer. In most ways he doesn't. No matter what the occasion, Carl always "has to work." He's always "busy," needing to "organize" his one-bedroom assisted living apartment. To organize, for him, literally means to move trinkets and half-torn boxes around this musty little place, hoping desperately to find rest. To find order in the chaos, safety in the paralyzing darkness—to see again.

Micah talked about Isaiah 53:11 as we lay in bed last night. I imagine it was interesting, but was honestly half-asleep and don't remember. This morning I looked it up again.

---

127 Psalm 55:6–8.

Out of the anguish of his soul he shall see and be satisfied;

by his knowledge shall the righteous one, my servant,

make many to be accounted righteous,

and he shall bear their iniquities.

An astounding prophecy about Jesus and this Lenten season, but today it makes me think about Carl. And motherhood. Out of the blind anguish of his soul, Father, you are healing Carl's ultimate sight. Tedious and stubborn though the process, you are teaching him to see and be satisfied.

Motherhood has felt like Carl's apartment. I move and remove and move again trinkets of "cha-cha-trains" and string cheese and trails of mud from cute yellow rain boots. It feels like messiness is my only option, and franticness in the messiness. Somewhere in it I know rest awaits, that praises can awaken in my thirtieth round of "head, shoulders, knees, and toes." And sometimes I find those prayers of restful praise. But usually I don't.

Maybe our views of worship have become too sanitized, too cleaned up. Prior to Jesus segueing our faith story into a "priesthood of all believers,"[128] Judaic worship involved gross engagements with the senses—sojourning by foot and donkey to the temple, smelling body odor and blood, watching smoke billow from the Temple.[129] Today we show up for an hour on Sunday mornings behind the safety of smiles and mascara. And Monday through Saturday, our busy search plows on, blind duty coercing and every wipe somehow further embittering. We swing between contentment and neurotic craving, forgetting no matter how organized our kitchen is, or polished we look from the outside, "my soul will be

---

128 See I Peter 2:5.
129 See Deuteronomy 12:27 and Joshua 22:27.

restless until she finds rest in Thee."[130] We forget duty isn't a trustworthy motivator; only love is.

David may've been sitting on my couch when he penned, "She is merely a moving shadow, and all her busy rushing ends in nothing."[131] I've been hoping lately to find a line in Ecclesiastes that reads, "There's a time[132] for haste and there's a time to smell the roses." The haste part just comes so naturally; *surely* it correlates with virtue, no?

Busyness is a sin of our day that's celebrated—posed as if a feature of godliness, even.

> *Being in a hurry. Getting to the next thing without fully entering the thing in front of me. I cannot think of a single advantage I've ever gained from being in a hurry. But a thousand broken and missed things, tens of thousands, lie in the wake of all the rushing.... Through all that haste I thought I was making up time. It turns out I was throwing it away.[133]*

Growth can be painstakingly slow; I get that. Studying a fetus, or seedling, or my soul, has told me so. But shouldn't salvation have affected our growth rates? Granted, God doesn't speak to me in audible sentences, but I tried envisioning what he might have said if he did.

Me: Trying not to judge, but just some observations here, Lord. Shouldn't you have lived at least to your nineties to make a real impact? And did you really mean to spend your last supper hanging out with merely twelve friends? Wouldn't a revival for twelve hundred, or twelve thousand, have been more fruitful? Even your era choice—might a more technologically

---

130 Paraphrase of Augustine of Hippo (354–430) in Confessions: "Our hearts are restless until they find rest in you."
131 Paraprhase of Psalm 39:6, New Living Translation.
132 See Ecclesiastes 3.
133 Mark Buchanan, *The Rest of God: Restoring Your Soul By Restoring Your Sabbath* (Nashville, TN: Nelson, 2007), 45.

savvy one have been a wiser move?

Him: Stay weak; it's where your strength is.

Me: I don't remember saying anything about weakness. I was talking about time.

Him: I know, dear daughter. Time actually has a lot to do with weakness. It convinces you that it needs a controller. A strong one. It convinces you that it's out of control, like a leaking faucet that will both run out of water and cause an unrepairable flood.

Me: So, explain the weak part again?

Him: Stay weak; it's where your strength is.[134]

Me: That makes no sense.

Him: I know. Well, I know it doesn't make sense to you, because I know time feels limited to you. Like there's a way out of it. Or it's gonna run out. Time scares you. It doesn't scare me though. I made it, I rule over it, I redeem it. The bare bones of creativity and creation and time are good and holy because I ordained them good and holy.[135] Time doesn't overwhelm me.

Me: Your confidence is refreshing. But it's not where I am.

Him: Be patient with yourself, darling, believing that patience is a fruit of my spirit.[136] Peace is too, no matter how rushed you feel. It's not natural

---

134 See II Corinthians 12:10.
135 See Genesis 2:3.
136 See Galatians 5:22.

for you to view time like I do. It's supernatural when time doesn't stress or enslave you. Few things have the capacity to muzzle your soul like time and thinking there isn't enough of it. "Open wide your mouth today, though, and I will fill it"[137] with meaning and grace and time enough to smell a delicate rose.

Me: Okay, I'll try to just focus on today. And stay weak. Thank you for your patience with me.

....

Dinner with friends last week led to conversations on Lent. One shared about giving up chocolate, another about prioritizing solitude in the place of social media. Part of the table landed on the side of, "I'm *beyond* that. Giving up things is for religious people, not those of us who understand grace. 'Sacrifices and offerings he has not desired.'"[138] The other part of the table suggested, "Maybe we should join, knowing that disciplines are a road to freedom. 'Whoever will lose his life shall find it.'"[139]

In my experience, laying something down, or doing something for God, isn't magic but an invitation to commune with God. And over time, communing with God changes us. Or God changes us as we commune with him. Same with Lent, I think. Lent isn't magic but a season with invitation to commune with God, maybe about discipline and boundaries, maybe about permission and learning freedom. And communing with God changes us. It looks with me at cracks in my life, not always to make them disappear, but to debilitate them a bit, or deepen understandings of their grip on me. Lent seems to lend perspective, noting views that could stand some clarifying, refreshers on who I am and am not, and the

---

137 See Psalm 81:10.
138 See Hebrews 10:5.
139 See Matthew 16:25.

extent to which he engages both. Lent steps me into the desert for forty days, facing thirsts and enemies, and emptying, not for the sake of gaining ground with God, but for the sake of becoming more grounded in his emptying love.

Gray-navy eyes searched my blue, as if for a quiet corner of the ocean after an exhausting storm. Eden's body was calm on my chest now, forehead nuzzled in my cheek. "He has set your feet in a broad place."[140] "Weeping may tarry for the night, but joy comes with the morning."[141] Moisture rolled from my eyes, as if Eden's tears had told them they were welcome. As if they had said, *"Home is not all the way here yet, and it's gonna be okay."* We laid in this gaze awhile. Then I served burnt lasagna and told Micah again that I loved him.

---

140 See Psalm 31:8.
141 Psalm 30:5b.

13. BELONGING

Brewing storm,

redecorating a room of creation

Pursuing,

not a millimeter without

breadth and length and height and depth

fierce enough to shatter a shadow

Space between,

waiting, watching, hoping

Grounding,

still, delicate, whole,

reaching up,

touching fringes of love

raining down

At any rate, as far as personal sorrows are concerned, it would be a very sharp and trying experience to me to think that I have an affliction which God never sent me—that the bitter cup was never filled by His hands, that my trials were never measured out by Him, nor sent to me by His arrangement of their weight and quantity. Oh, that would be bitterness indeed!

—Charles Spurgeon, "Woe and Weal" [142]

---

142 Charles H. Spurgeon, "Woe and Weal" in *The Metropolitan Tabernacle Pulpit Sermons* (vol. 57; London: Passmore & Alabaster, 1911), 99–100.

"I suppose it's not that I don't have the time or energy to write at this point; I just don't know what I would say." The journal listened sympathetically. "My life is feels predominantly *little*. I'm with little ones most hours of most days."

At some point in my life I felt successful because I made straight A's, or won a tennis tournament. At another because I had a date, or finished a marathon. Currently I feel successful because my daughter got half her poop in the toilet.

Are you saying your life feels little right now? a quiet voice within me queried.[143]

"I don't think so... but maybe... I guess so? Okay, yes. My days can feel little in the sense of significance. Little in the sense of how much is happening aside from potty training and repetitions of 'ba.' But I know better; I know that mothering is a phenomenal form of discipleship. I know that little ones are a primary path to the Kingdom and of matchless priority to Jesus."[144]

It doesn't sound like you feel that way though, the quiet voice gently searched again.

"No. You're right. I don't usually feel that way. Instead I feel like an hour alone at Kroger staring at cheese options would be comparable to a vacation in Hawaii."

Success apparently takes on new definitions with new seasons. And God has me in a new season. There's a saying, sometimes attributed to Mother

---

143 See Psalm 139:23–24.
144 See Matthew 18:3.

Teresa, "If you want to bring happiness to the world, go home and love your family."[145] Part of me gives a hearty amen to this; part of me resists it. It's hard not to rate this season as less fruitful than seasons past, where productivity felt high or relational impact wide. It's hard to deem my days "successful," or justify how a ministry that fits into a crib is "fruitful."

Part of me is not wanting to surrender to where God has me, still wanting the free-spirited, nose-studded single life that travels and hikes and writes in coffee shops. Not the one who's usually at home in sweat pants, doing laundry, trying to cook an edible meal, or kiss a "huut knee." Part of me struggles to know these roles as holy, as worship.

One of the few imperatives Scripture speaks about children is that they are a blessing. Culture doesn't tend to view them this way; it's the nose-studded traveler, living the high life with utmost freedom that they esteem. Or the woman who's figured out how to "balance" full-time motherhood with a full-time job with full-time roles on the PTA, Girl-Scout, and city-council boards. What about staying at home with my children? Can that be enough—a means to communion with Christ, even? Can the Trinity really be present, speaking, sanctifying, and glorifying in a diaper change, or repetitions of "ba"?[146]

....

Being a stay-at-home mom runs deep in my story. Before societal, or parental, or theological voices shared their views, it was my dream. A boisterous dinner table and tucking love notes into lunch boxes felt like part of my design, part of myself that I someday hoped to meet. As I field my seventeenth request for crackers at 8:40 a.m., I realize I'm meeting her.

---

145 *New World Encyclopedia*, s.v. "Mother Teresa," accessed June 9, 2017, http://www. newworldencyclopedia.org/entry/Mother_Teresa.
146 For the record, I still have the nose stud.

My son coos beside me; my daughter is entrenched in the coloring book. I stalk Instagram while pans wait patiently on the counter. In some ways, the stay-at-home mom is just who I envisioned: satisfying, engaged, alive. In other ways, she's not. Her days are more busy and mundane than I envisioned, more simple and somehow chaotic, running a jagged course I never knew possible, with meaningful highs and naked lows.

I've started to wonder, *Is being a stay-at-home mom enough? Is just being at home with my children today satisfactory?* If so, why the tension, and how did "just" enter the conversation? No one says, "I'm *just* a teacher," or *"just* a doctor." Women aren't expected to stay at home anymore. It's not the norm to "just" be a mother. Even for us stay-at-home moms (and even when finances don't deem it necessary), there's a pull toward *also* being an essential oils rep, writing a cookbook, or creating a blog that influences the masses. Who are "the masses" anyway?

I reflect on my grandmothers, both versions of June Cleaver in my memories, draped with an apron, jotting a thank-you note for the potluck last week. *Did these women have layers beneath? What did they worry about, or talk about on playdates? Did they ever feel teased by unavailable pursuits— wrestle with their job at home not being enough?* Or I think about my own mother, remembering how I watched her reflection in the mirror, diagonal strokes blushing her subtle cheekbones before the babysitter arrived. *How much will be enough to gain mommy's delight?* I wondered. Through adolescence and into adulthood, journal entries repeated a variation. *Will I ever be enough to capture a man's affection? Am I enough, God, to capture your attention?* With two down for naps and an empty page before me, I'm still pondering "enough." When will it be satisfied, and why does it so quickly lead as my barometer of (lacking) peace?

If I read them a bedtime story, or the red bump on her eye goes away? If he doesn't roll off the bed again, or if I check off "exercise, clean, and cook" and maintain joy amidst meltdowns, enthusiasm toward afternoon boredom—then have I done enough? If Micah comes home to savory aromas and a well-behaved household, have I done my job well?

The voice of "enough" tells me, "No. There is yet more. Always. That was kind of you to remember her birthday, but why not write a letter instead of just an email. Glad you found the deal on salmon, but how about finding a coupon for the other ten things, too. You should at least have time to steam mop and bake muffins for the neighbors across the street. Oh and you missed a spot when shaving your legs this morning. And when you finish these, come back. I always have more to offer." Clearly "enough" will never be satisfied. Should it remain my barometer, I will never know peace.

Sometimes I think my "enough" questions are about guilt. There's a story in John 8 where Jesus is teaching in the temple. Some studied religious folks bring him a woman who'd cheated on her husband. Angrily pushing her through the crowds, they yell, "Teacher, this woman has been caught in the act of adultery. Now in the Law, Moses commanded us to stone such women. So what do you say?" Jesus knelt down and starts writing on the ground with his finger. They keep badgering him for an answer. He replies, "Let him who is without sin among you be the first to throw a stone at her." One by one they walk away until it is just Jesus and the woman. He asks her, "Woman, where are they? Has no one condemned you?" She says, "No one, Lord." So he says to her, "Neither do I condemn you; go, and from now on sin no more."[147] We don't know what Jesus scribed in the sand, but it alludes to words that knocked the breath out of this woman's shame. And rightfully shamed the arrogance of those

---

147 See John 8:1–4.

breathing down her throat. It alludes to guilt—forgiving guilt, telling guilt it has no place anymore.

I also think my "enough" questions can be about boredom. A therapist once defined boredom to me as the inability to enjoy oneself. When I'm enjoying myself, the self God has thoughtfully given to me, I feel free. I feel awake and alive. I feel honored to be a mother who gets to spend full days at home with her children, and I feel free to be a mother who in a given day does this, or doesn't do this, but *gets to be with* her children.

My thoughts drift to the lovely lines read at many wedding ceremonies, the ones about love being patient and kind, not envying or boasting, not arrogant or rude. The ones about love not insisting on its own way, not being irritable or resentful, nor rejoicing at wrongdoing, but rejoicing with the truth. Bearing all things, believing all things, hoping all things, enduring all things.[148] I daresay they're some of the most illuminating and challenging words of the entire Bible. My soul ain't feelin' lovely though. Rather, frustrated, pitiable, weighed down by resentment. I don't want to run simply because my season is hard, though, or scramble to find relief simply because I fear missing out or misery within.

How did you endure, Jesus? How did you not doubt your significance when you were weary? Your calling, Lord, in the midnight hours? You were "a man of sorrows and acquainted with grief."[149] You labored to the utmost, nail marks puncturing your sweating palms, stabbing accusations and stretching horrific holes through your extremities—marks through your fragile limbs.

John 15:5 comes to mind, where Jesus says, "I am the vine; you are the branches. Whoever abides in me and I in him, he it is that bears much fruit, for apart from me you can do nothing." Maybe abiding in Jesus

---

148 See I Corinthians 13:4–7.
149 Isaiah 53.3.

is our greatest goal as moms; maybe it's our barometer for success. And maybe our scope of mothering is too narrow, too tied to the severing of an umbilical cord. Maybe femininity and motherhood, being and becoming a woman, maybe these branches don't fit into a crib—aren't supposed to fit into a crib. Maybe they are vast and brilliantly complex, growing beyond a definable space. In the words of Ann Voskamp, maybe "Motherhood is a calling to come closer, not a command to be more."[150]

I learned as a single person that motherhood is wider than biology. Late to the altar, I had considered that maybe I was called instead to the celibate life as a missionary in Africa. I wrote a book about this,[151] even, but am still trying to believe it's true. Paul shares a radical theology of parenting—spiritual parenting—where going and making disciples transcends marriage and sex and babies.[152] Likewise, Jesus emphasizes God as our ultimate parent[153] and a Kingdom family[154] primary to the nuclear one.

Amy Carmichael, unmarried missionary to India in the early 20th century, traveled often to distant villages meeting diverse needs. Over time, her call crystallized to mothering "temple babies," enslaved from infancy to dark sides of Hinduism. This Amma (Mamma) wrestled with feeling pinned down, "unspiritual," and less productive than in former days. But at the same time, she was "beginning to see that she must allow her feet to be tied 'for the sake of Him whose feet once were nailed.'"[155]

150 Ann Voskamp, "How to catch a falling star: an adoption story [or why you thought you should not adopt or care for an orphan— and were wrong]," *Ann Voskamp*, accessed June 9, 2017, http://annvoskamp.com/2016/06/how-to-catch-a-falling-star-an-adoption-story-or-why-you-thought-should-not-adopt-or-care-for-an-orphan-and-were-wrong/
151 *Celibate Sex: Musings on Being Loved, Single, Twisted, and Holy* (Colorado Springs, CO: Navpress, 2010).
152 See I Corinthians 4:14–15.
153 See Matthew 23:9.
154 See Luke 8:19–21.
155 Elisabeth Elliot, *A Chance to Die: The Life and Legacy of Amy Carmichael* (Grand Rapids, MI: Revell, 1987), 178.

I long to be a part of the adventurous, valuable Commission to "go and make disciples."[156] But maybe going and making entails a willingness to *stay and be made.* Maybe investing in my children throughout the day *is* a fulfillment of Jesus' words in Matthew 28. Maybe *they* are my great commission this season. Day in and day out, maybe *they* are my most radical investment of discipleship, those to whom I've been entrusted to tell the Good News of God's love.[157] "Hate not laborious work,"[158] Amy said, "joy, joy is in it."[159]

If the Lord of Glory took a towel and knelt on the floor to wash the dusty feet of His disciples (the job of the lowest slave in an Eastern household), then no work, even the relentless and often messy routine of caring for squalling babies, is demeaning. To offer it up to the Lord of Glory transforms it into a holy task. "Could it be right," Amy had asked, "to turn from so much that might be of profit and become just nursemaids?" The answer was yes. It is not the business of the servant to decide which work is great, which is small, which is important or unimportant—he is not greater than his master. "If by doing some work which the undiscerning consider 'not spiritual work' I can best help others, and I inwardly rebel, thinking it is the spiritual for which I crave, when in truth it is the interesting and exciting, then I know nothing of Calvary love."[160]

Maybe stretch marks have more to do with nail marks, and nail marks more to do with stretch marks, and love, than we account for. Maybe stretch marks prepare a way for resurrection. Maybe stretch marks are about Jesus, "...who for the joy that was set before him endured the cross, despising the shame, and is seated at the right hand of the throne of

---

156 See Matthew 28:16-20.
157 Thankful for this reminder that rainy morning on 36th Street, Victoria.
158 Ecclesiasticus (Apocrypha)
159 Amy Carmichael, "Finding Joy," in *Mountain Breezes: The Collected Poems of Amy Carmichael*, ed. Elisabeth Elliot (Fort Washington: CLC Publications, 2013), lines 1-2.
160 Ibid. 182-83.

God."[161]

...like a root out of dry ground;

he had no form or majesty that we should look at him,

and no beauty that we should desire him.

He was despised and rejected by men,

a man of sorrows, and acquainted with grief;

and as one from whom men hide their faces

he was despised, and we esteemed him not.

—Isaiah 53:2–4

When peers provoked Jesus with "enough" questions ("How much is enough to get me to heaven?" or "Who's doing enough to become the greatest?"), he knew "enough answers" would never be enough. He knew the souls of his children are only satisfied with Immanuel. This name of Jesus is mentioned three times in Scripture and translates to "God with us" or God in our midst. With us in the broken animal crackers and rocking chairs and onesies a size too small. To the guilt and should of "enough," that is, you can "Devise your strategy, but it will be thwarted; propose your plan, but it will not stand, for God is with us."[162]

Tending to the dishes tonight, Elliana nuzzled up against the back of my knees. Not a pushy or whiney nuzzle, but a nuzzle that felt more about belonging, an unspoken sentence that she *wanted to be with.*

God, would you help me be present with my children, noticing their eyes and

---

161 See Hebrews 12:1-2.
162 Isaiah 8:10, (NIV).

listening for you in their play? Would you help me surrender the part of me that wants to be enough for them? I can't be enough, or do enough, or give enough to rescue someone, to understand and fix and heal the broken stories in their inner and outer midsts, but I still try. Would you help me remember my greatest task, Immanuel, is to be with you? You left your home to be with us, that we might learn to be with you. Please teach me to be at home in you, that I might truly be with my children. And to believe being at home with my children, as an overflow of being at home with you, is more than enough. Amen.

14. SAFE

Unless I see in his hands the mark of the nails, and place my finger into the mark of the nails, and place my hand into his side, I will never believe.

—*John 20:25b*

He who has a why to live for can bear almost any how.

—*Friedrich Nietzsche*[163]

163 "Maxims and Arrows," in *Twilight of the Idols*, accessed June 9, 2017, http://www. handprint.com/SC/NIE/GotDamer.html#sect1

Some days I have an easier time believing God. Today wasn't one of them. I woke in a bad mood. Had gone to bed in a bad mood, too, but expected the night to ease my mind. It didn't. Book sales have crept-in as my new bathroom scale. Whereas I used to blame my singleness, or entire significance, on a number on that dinky glass square, now I do it to with numbers of books sold.

I've waited to come across something in Scripture like, "Dearest Abbie, even though Amazon sales didn't love you this week, I still do." Never found it, or anything half-related. I used to get annoyed that God never mentioned my dating life in Scripture either, or my weight. I wanted him to care as much about them as I did, and provide a solution. Or worthy penance. Instead, I feel as though his words translate in my vernacular as more along the lines of, "Abbie, dear, trust my process; it is love. I care more about you and every hair on your head than you can imagine. I've begun a good work in you and won't let up until my radiant image has been restored fully in yours. Your worth is not in a number, or another person. It is in me; you are significant because you are mine, bought at a mighty price, and never to be sold back. You cannot alter how I adore you." Again, just wish I believed all this at a core level.

I also woke hungry. And not just any hungry, but picky hungry, like for a particular peanut-butter bar, only found at a particular store ten minutes away. Somewhere en route, I started reflecting on summer and how I enjoy this season because of its lack of structure, but also how weary I can become by lack of structure. My mind floated between different times in my life where neurotic structure defined me, or when anything half-related to structure was obliterated. Then I recalled a bizarre season striking something in the middle.

It was during a nine-month journey through the Spiritual Exercises of Saint Ignatius. There are loads of resources on in the ins and outs of this retreat, but in short, it entails an intentional hour spent with God each day. Parts of the time are structured; every day has a prescribed hour-long course of meditation. But parts are unstructured; how one shows up, or how a given day's course shows up, is up to God.

Each month, I would meet with a ninety-year-old nun/spiritual director to talk about the process. She was calm and gentle and made me feel safe. One time she told me I could throw away my journal entries. Particularly the crass, nasty ones that tend to start with an F that you're scared to admit are from your heart and scared to write down. "Just tear it up and burn it, or flush it down the toilet," she said, without a hint of shame or childish accusation. It's been some of the most liberating counsel I've ever received.

I'm not sure how I feel about this ethically, but some of Mother Teresa's private journals were published after her death.[164] Let's just say, it's not the Mother Teresa you grew up hearing about. Her journals expose painful depths of doubt and wrestling. Reading through them, however, Teresa became no longer a distant saint, but a sister with whom I shared common ground. Likewise, throughout my year working through the Exercises, I learned healing doesn't happen when ink, or my heart and beliefs, shape themselves properly or prettily. Healing happens in learning to hear God's love for me, even when I've fallen. Or maybe especially when I've fallen. It isn't about learning not to fall off my bike anymore, but learning the tools to get back on when falling happens. Ways to cope with Christ through and after the Fall.

---

164 Mother Teresa: *Come Be My Light: The Private Writings of the Saint of Calcutta.* Ed. Brian Kolodieichuk (Image, 2009).

By this point I'd made it to store and gathered my peanut butter bar. Thoughts had turned to something like, "God, help me be open to your views on structure this season." I proceeded to check out, which is where you'll think I'm starting to lie, or use authorial liberties, but I swear on my life, I'm not. Two nuns walked through the door. Granted, they weren't Jesuits (nuns of the Ignatian order), but come on. Have you ever seen two nuns at the grocery store, especially when you were thinking about nuns five minutes earlier?

Nuns are surely used to being stared at, but the length of my stare was probably a little awkward. Tranquil smiles beamed back. And that was it. I went to my car and they… went shopping, I guess (do nuns really buy groceries?). No exact answers, or miraculous mood-shifters, and yet, a meaningful answer and space for my shifting mood. It was as if God was affirming that I was allowed to struggle with changes of season, or a sloppy relationship with structure. It was as if He was saying, "Abbie, with every gain comes a loss and every lost season, a gain. Through it all though, I am near. You just be you, and I'll just be me, and we're gonna be alright." Apparently I'm not the kind who rolls out of bed with belief. I need evident reminders, like nuns at the grocery store, or else he and I both know I'll stop believing.

....

Whole wheat bunnies crunched nervously between my molars. I drove too fast and smelled like urine; morning jogs and my pelvic floor haven't become friends again since childbirth.

The day had begun lovely, rising early with Micah to share an unexpected 4th anniversary dawn. Words from Moses summarize our sentiments:

"You have led in steadfast love the people whom you have redeemed; you have guided them by your strength to your holy abode."[165] Then a "thud" came from the back room—where Eden was. Where hadn't-rolled-over-yet Eden had lain contentedly on the bed, surrounded by fluffy pillows.

Micah sprinted. I hesitantly followed, fearing the scene before me. Eden lay upside down, stuck between a wider than usual gap between the mattress and headboard. The five-ish seconds from couch to arms were long and silent. Dreadfully silent. Eden screamed, as his papa's hands scooped down to retrieve him. I shuddered, reaching for my baby boy, calming him, trying to calm myself, with the words of "Holy, Holy, Holy." He seemed okay, but I still drove to the pediatrician's office, too fast and smelling like urine from my unhealed lady parts.

"He's fine," the doctor assured me, "and I can pretty much guarantee this won't be the last time." Oh the smothering love of a parent for a child, the love so deep it hurts. Yes, I reminded myself, *he leads in steadfast love; he guides them by his strength to his holy abode.*

Turns out I had given the pediatrician the wrong date for Eden's birthday. Didn't realize it until driving home. My brain feels like the chunky kid who gets a hit, but can't make it to first base, *ever.* Or remember splatter paint as a kid? I think I had four birthday parties based on it. That's my emotional dashboard: different colors and shapes and chaos All. Over. The page.

It's not that I'm at a loss for thoughts. Their eruptions and calm musings cradle me throughout the day, but they rarely move beyond a cordial hello. Too many other needs are begging my attention; jotting down thoughts, better yet a coherent strand of them, feels foreign. I miss this luxury.

---

165 Exodus 15:13.

At bite two of runny eggs from the frying pan, I heard the vital announcement that, "Eeeedin cwwying" (while he should be REMing). As if I didn't hear. A couple hours later, "Mummy, fugger culur" (fingers color), Elliana squealed, skipping around the bedroom with a Sharpie as I acquainted myself with pumping on one side and nursing on the other. Bad idea. I squirted. He choked. She laughed. Sharpie swayed like a magic wand, pronouncing freedom and newfound independence. I snapped. He spit up. She had a meltdown. And we're all hoping "fugger" doesn't make a public debut.

....

"New neighbors moved in and I've yet to invite them for a meal."

"Old neighbors still live there and I've not invited them for a meal in too long."

"Forgot to call her back. Crap, also forgot to turn the oven on."

"She's been wanting to get together for weeks."

Laundry, poop, breathe, grocery, wash dishes, prioritize husband, change diaper, add Cascade to grocery list, decide on a dinner, shower (maybe), clean spit-up, put down for naps, pay bills, return call, decide on another dinner because you don't have black beans, give baths, schedule appointment, put away dishes...

"Crap, I didn't turn the oven off."

These sporadic thoughts invade my mind *all day long.* I attempt to label them with an emotion or response: "Frustration, laughter, bitterness, loss of control, resentment, loneliness, guilt, fatigue, joy, fear, grief, hope, longing, anger, childlike sentiments, geriatric sentiments..." I run out of space. I swear I could flood our house if someone ever pricked my brain.

The margin is slim, and the little margin I do have feels squished. My parents gave me a membership to the YMCA for Christmas. I've dropped the kids twice already this week at childcare and gone to sit in the toilet stall for ten minutes, just because I can. Just because I know I won't be interrupted there.

See, I'm not an interruption kind of gal. I'm an introverted, controlled, controller. I can stand noise for only so long before I crave a dark closet. I make lists that play out plans by the hour. Or so I did. Internally I may be swirling, but externally I'm usually relatively together. Or so I was. Now my wardrobe is mostly sweats, and my kids' wardrobe is mostly diapers. Thoughts rarely progress into complete sentences. I'm not drowning, but I'm definitely treading water. At some existential level, I know the water is holding me up, somehow even moving me somewhere, but I'm clueless as to much beyond that.

An agent wrote last week, inquiring about projects I'm working on. It felt like that time when you weren't interested in him, but it still felt good to be hit on. I wish I could be interested. But it's just not where I am right now. Writing is an identity I cling to, an idol I often flirt with. But it's not whom I'm to treasure these hours. I have a husband and babies who long for that treasuring-in. A Christ who does, too. As the age old question wonders, while treading, while serving as a chaotically-minded wife, mommy, and daughter of the King? How shall I order my affections while repetitively making my way through six loads of laundry and 74 high-pitched pleas for "wa-wa" (water) and fugger culurs?

Today I attempt to write from where I am, a screen full of unsanitized fingerprints and the dim features of a new book. My last book sold, like, three copies, yet here I go again. To be a writer, apparently, is to keep writing. To keep standing in margins, looking toward a space unknown, attempting a language of creation, of procreation. Attempting a language of belief. To be a writer, apparently, is to participate with surrender, to wait for words… to listen, and then to tell. In weakness and in strength, in sickness and in health, the meaningful story before you. To be a writer, apparently, is to be brave. *Here I am. Please, Lord, speak.*

> *Open my ear to grasp quickly thy Spirit's voice,*
>
> *and delightfully run after his beckoning hand;*
>
> *Melt my conscience that no hardness remain,*
>
> *make it alive to evil's slightest touch;*
>
> *When Satan approaches may I flee to thy wounds,*
>
> *and there cease to tremble at all alarms.*[166]

---

166 "Need of Jesus," in *The Valley of Vision: A Collection of Puritan Prayers and Devotions.* Ed. Arthur Bennett (Carlisle: Banner of Truth Trust, 2009), 102.

15. NOISE

What will you do in the mundane days of faithfulness?

—Martin Luther

Every day we experience something of the death of the Lord Jesus, so that we may also know the power of the life of Jesus in these bodies of ours.

—II Corinthians 4:10 (Phillips)

You know it's bad when vacuum sounds bring reprieve. Tired of snot and fuss and clingy babies, I binged on gummy vitamins and neurotically tried to de-crumb my floor.

Sometimes I hear crying that doesn't exist. Racing through a shower this morning, dopamine convinced me that hearing only the rushing water meant child number one must've lugged child number two either into the street or onto the dock. Wrapped in a towel, having cut my shower short, the true story I found was two babies on the floor mat flipping through *Frog and Toad*. Everyone tells me it's a season that will pass.

My friend Brian used to talk about how petrified he was of going on retreat, of getting alone with God. Namely for reasons of hearing him, or maybe more terrifyingly, *not* hearing him. Hearing from God paralyzes some of us. What if he says, "Sell your favorite everything, move to the bush to tell people how good God is." But on the other hand, what if he just wants to say "Good morning"?

I ponder "voice" as a liturgy of words escapes through the cracks in my daughter's crib.

"Howse. Daddy. Cheese. Mummy's howse. Kiss. Keeys. Ee-den."

Elliana's voice is distinctly feminine and cute enough to tie in a bow. Rarely does it pause, as if enchanted by too much goodness to fit everything into a day's worth of words. From wake to sleep, clips from a story roll from her lively imagination.

"Pray… daddy, eeeat, Bailey, Bailey's house, Mummy, eye, nose, a-b-c-h-i-j… auuumen."

"Papa... tweet-tweet-tweet... Toes. One-tree-four-siiix. Tree. Book. Chawk. Burd's howse..."

Eden has only "coo" and "bah." *What will his voice say? What is the story his voice will tell the world? What is my voice? What story am I telling the world? Does our family have a voice?*

He stares through a kitchen window pane, fixated on patterns of the rain. I write from Gmail instead of a Word document; it's easier to click "compose" and feel connected via email than engage an open document. Usually I like the solitude that comes from the drastically white, empty page. Today I don't. Beneath gazes of joy as she unraveled Christmas bows, Elliana's eyes told me parts of her are still jealous. Eight months into Eden, she's still not convinced the garden is again secure.

The hardest part of the weeks following his birth involved tending to her emotions. Adorned with raw nipples and grey bags under my eyes, I needed to make her understand it was going to be okay. That mommy could still make it to her every tear and crushed goldfish cracker. It's taken a lot of months to let go of this tedious lie, the one that assures me incessantly that I can be the Savior of my child's world. *Have mothers throughout history felt this tension? Did Mary feel a proclivity toward rescuing Jesus from every hurt?* At some level I knew a sibling would be good for Elliana. At some level I know it's an early invitation toward the Gospel, toward knowing life does not revolve around us, and that the only One who can meet our every need is Jesus. It doesn't feel this way right now. Heartbreak and pain seem more tangible.

The apostle Paul says if the resurrection wasn't a reality, Jesus is a waste of our time.[167] Restoration would be a waste of our belief. But if the words

---

167 I Corinthians 15:12-19.

of God are true, it is always his will to make new, writing restoration into every waking moment of our existence. Yesterday I sat on the porch with a friend who had miscarried. A baby and her drunk mother passed by on an empty street corner. Confusion felt more trustworthy than God. Verbally I dumped my load on Jesus. I don't want to carry it anymore. The word "restoration" came to mind. *"Why this word, Lord? I don't know what it means. I don't know how it correlates with me, or you, or this hour. I don't know how to believe this aspect of your being."* Restoration. Those eleven letters stayed with me on my ride home. Restoration. Restorative. Restoring. When? Restoring what? *When will you restore restoration?* What is restoration? Arriving home I looked it up. Turns out "restore" shows up 126 times in Scripture. These were some that stood out:

But now for a brief moment grace has been shown from the LORD our God, to leave us an escaped remnant and to give us a peg in His holy place, that our God may enlighten our eyes and grant us a little reviving in our bondage. For we are slaves; yet in our bondage our God has not forsaken us, but has extended loving-kindness to us in the sight of the kings of Persia, to give us reviving to raise up the house of our God, to restore its ruins and to give us a wall in Judah and Jerusalem.

—Ezra 9:8–10 (NASB)

If you return to the Almighty, you will be restored...

—Job 22:23a (NIV)

He restores my soul.

—Psalm 23:3a

In the time of my favor I will answer you,

and in the day of salvation I will help you;

I will keep you and will make you

to be a covenant for the people,

to restore the land

and to reassign its desolate inheritances...

—Isaiah 49:8 (NIV)

The people were amazed when they saw the mute speaking, the crippled made well, the lame walking and the blind seeing. And they praised the God of Israel.

—Matthew 15:31 (NIV)

Then Jesus laid his hands on his eyes again; and he opened his eyes, his sight was restored, and he saw everything clearly.

—Mark 8:25

Restore us to You, O LORD, that we may be restored...

—Lamentations 5:21 (NASB)

Restore to me the joy of your salvation, and uphold me with a willing spirit.

—Psalm 51:12

It seems God's ideas and styles of restoration are different from mine. I like to start with good and try and make it better; he likes to start with nothing and make it whole. He likes to breathe life into vacancy, and love into the damaged soul, creating anew, cooperating with our new creation, causing our hearts to be mended.

....

It's six days after the 25th, but I can't bring myself to finalize the season, to move beyond the birth part, or reconcile the death part. Tree clippings still adorn our fireplace, and lights from the (maybe-next-year-we'll-step-up-to-a-tree) bush in the corner. The week before New Year's makes me crazy. At the drop of a chilly, sparkly apple tonight, poof, this year will disappear.

In *The Problem of Pain,* C.S. Lewis writes that "pain insists upon being attended to. God whispers to us in our pleasures, speaks in our conscience, but shouts in our pain; it is His megaphone to rouse a deaf world."[168] A baby pushed himself out of my body this year. Labor pains were my megaphone.

I get that Christmas is about birth—new birth—God dwelt ("tabernacled" says the Greek) among us birth. But the week after Christmas feels palpably like death to me. Whereas the weeks building into Advent feel pregnant, this week following feels hollow and disillusioned, like a deer staring into headlights.

She had the baby. Now what? The pregnancy of Advent gave us reason to wait. There were tangible conclusions for which we were waiting. The story of Christmas lent reason to decorate and prepare and feast. And then it happened. He was born; Immanuel, God *with* us. We feasted more, savoring the gift. Presents and presence, nestled in knowing. But then the time came, to leave the manger, to sweep up evergreen aromas. The womb feels *without* again, the year ahead unknown. Maybe Jesus is

---

168 C.S. Lewis, *The Problem of Pain* (San Francisco, CA: HarperCollins, 2001), 93.

easier to trust in a pregnant story? Maybe he's easier to fathom with all the songs and light and magic of the season. As a real, born person, maybe Jesus can be harder to grab hold of, following him more complex.

We had to cancel twice on friends coming for dinner a few weeks ago. Then Eden was asked to be baby Jesus in the nativity play. Elliana was already set to be a sheep and a tad underage for the role, and I assumed she'd be a wandering, frightened one (turns out she was). Envisioning Eden freaking out (turns out he didn't) as teeny-boppers Mary, Joseph, and Gabriel passed him around was too much, too unpredictable, too beyond one's ability to depend on me, or on my children, to act "correctly" (as if sheep don't wander, or baby Jesus didn't wail at random or unexpected times). When did I grow up anyway, get married, and have not just have one, but two children eligible to be part of a Nativity play?

I dropped them off at my parents' for a few hours. The ride home felt hollow, mimicking the lonely float of this week between Christmas and New Year's, where time bends you between a bizarre fog of sadness and hope. I want to be quiet; I want to still my soul from baby chatter; I want to contemplate God's benevolent presence. I want to be with my Lover without words, without the angst of explaining myself, unraveling myself, understanding myself. But that's not where I am. My soul is full of chatter and fog and wobbly attachments toward end and beginning, old year and new, past and coming. My present is between. But even here, I'm choosing to believe, his presence is present. And I mustn't be where I am not.

Tender Jesus, will you help me be here these minutes? Will you help me stay in the fog? Let us not run from this past year's pains, or settle too comfortably in its pleasures. Let us not fend off pain in the year to come, or shy away from its bounty of pleasures. Let us hear the megaphones. Let us rejoice in a God who speaks. Let us hear. Let us rejoice.

Yes, pain insists upon being attended to.

These children are mine, Father, but first they are yours. Thanks be to you, Christ, the inexpressible gift, swaddled amidst barn odors and the fragile sounds of exhaustion and hope. Whatever it takes today, whether vacuum cleaners, or children acting utterly out of character in a nativity play, would you help me hear your voice? Would you help me notice the noisy graces of your presence?

16. TENT

Question: What is your only comfort in in life and in death?

Answer: That I am not my own, but belong—body and soul, in life and in death—to my faithful Savior, Jesus Christ.

—Heidelberg Catechism Q & A 1

The Lord wraps himself in light as with a garment; he stretches out the heavens like a tent.

—Psalm 104:2 (NIV)

Epsom salt glistens in the enthusiastic stream. I sip from a curvaceous glass of red, dabble some drops of lavender, and start to recline into the hot suds. Instead I hit a stupid plastic boat. "They're long days, but short years," I try to remind myself.

I want to find God in the mundane, I really do, in the flossing and folding and chopping of cucumbers. I want to know as a sacred rhythm the scrubbing of eggplant grime. Frankly though, tonight it all just feels repetitive and meaningless. I smelled like Eden's diaper today, and I know the cashier knew it. She politely rung up my dozen eggs anyway. Words aren't making sense in my head or on paper. God isn't making sense. Something in me knows amidst absence we find true presence. And lacking words are invitations to found ones. But right now that sounds like flowery poetry that isn't true.

Being a writer sucks when no words come to your mind. *Did I do this? Did karma do this? But I don't believe in karma. But how does creativity flow vigorously for weeks at a time, imaginary and childlike, inspired and alive? And then cease. Just like that. Silent. Nada. Nothing.* When we have nothing to write about we either make stuff up or refurbish old stuff. Even if it's short, or dull, or apparently about nothing, I'm starting to think it's during these writing blocks that we really need to write. Because there really is no such thing as nothing, and nothing is always a bridge to something. Or at least that's the flowery poem I'm telling myself today.

I guess it's in these hours when I'm asked whether grace is really true. Grace toward myself. Grace to be weak. Grace to believe that in all things, in blocks and on bridges, in fullness and in voids, in rest and exhaustion, in plainness and the unlovely, that God is at work. Maybe tomorrow my block will dissipate, or I'll have something creative to say. Today, however, my aim is simply to write, even if apparently about nothing.

"You have kept count of my tossings; put my tears in your bottle."[169] Came across this verse from the Psalms during nap time. It first struck me in its compassion. Then in word choice. "Bottle" is in the Bible? And "tears in your bottle"—really? A bit cliché, Nicholas Sparks-y, no? I checked a few translations and they agreed with ESV's. So I guess it's true: *God puts our tears in His bottle.* No tear goes unnoticed or untended to. Good to know.

Come to me, all who labor and are heavy laden, and I will give you rest.

—Matthew 11:28

....

The mirror chuckled at my dilapidated nipples. Eden nursed for the last time at dawn. Part of me grieves a season's anticlimactic finale. Though feedings lately were a mere handful of mostly asleep 5am minutes, they're some of the most tender and intimate I've known. I am sad. And we're moving. Or actually already moved, but to a temporary space until Micah readies the permanent one. We're on heartbreak hill of a renovation that's lasted three times longer than expected. Ninety-nine percent of the time, I've learned, this is the case with reconstruction, but my heart still dives trustingly into the lap of the projected date, only to get dropped on her arse seventy-six times. (Micah spent five years renovating our last house. I don't care how stunning the projects look in the end; I officially hate them.) I keep thinking maybe if I scream loud enough into my pillow, sander and screw gun sounds will go away. They haven't yet.

It's been a "without" season, stripped of simple (first-world) luxuries like a second car, internet, washer and dryer, dishwasher, or breathing room

---

169 Psalm 56:8.

in our 600 square foot cottage. In virtuous theory, it's stripped us to the simple realities of our souls; in reality it's just made me grumpy. Hope deferred has made my heart grow sick.[170]

My mother's driving me batty, my mother-in-law is driving me more batty, and I miss 36th Street. It's where we first made love. It's where we first did taxes together, and decorated a Christmas tree; it's where I nursed our first child, and then our second; it's where we struggled through role differences and that renovation, and dreamed about running a retreat center someday. The crazy thing is, that dream is why we've moved. In God's brilliant orchestrations, we're getting to do what we dreamed of in many ways, running 130 acres known as Wesley Gardens Retreat. My soul has yet to catch up with the physical shift, though.

36th Street is where "loving my neighbor" became real. We were the minority, and one of the few not on welfare. "Family" on those streets tends to mean a single mom with four kids and four unknown or jailed dads. These dears became part of our family, whether checking fractions at afternoon tutoring, or having a beer with "Auntie Yolanda," an atheist public defender from Mexico whose dog Bailey annoyingly pooped in our shared yard.

I'm going to miss the immediacy of need. The immediacy of poverty and desperation and injustice. These realities can be hard to come by in America, glossed with space enough to pretend they don't exist. Oh how I long to continue seeing it. And seeing myself in it. Searching for hope in inner-city trenches. Cognizant of brokenness in outer-city spaces, on playgrounds and dinner tables, in churches and tree houses, in the pagan soul and the saved one. Frederich Buechner defines *calling*, saying, "The place God calls you to is the place where your deep gladness and the

---

170 See Proverbs 13:12.

world's deep hunger meet."[171] I long to keep searching for this calling.

Blessed are the poor in spirit, for theirs is the kingdom of heaven.

Blessed are those who mourn, for they shall be comforted.

Blessed are the meek, for they shall inherit the earth.

Blessed are those who hunger and thirst for righteousness, for they shall be satisfied.

Blessed are the merciful, for they shall receive mercy.

Blessed are the pure in heart, for they shall see God.

Blessed are the peacemakers, for they shall be called sons of God.

Blessed are those who are persecuted for righteousness' sake, for theirs is the kingdom of heaven.

Blessed are you when others revile you and persecute you and utter all kinds of evil against you falsely on my account. Rejoice and be glad, for your reward is great in heaven, for so they persecuted the prophets who were before you.

—Matthew 5:3–12

Two years ago I met a friend who's addicted to drugs and stuck in prostitution. Overall, her progress has been good, but last night she called to say she loved me, but life had taken its toll and she'd had enough. This week alone, her seventeen-year-old daughter found out she's pregnant; her twenty-year-old is cutting herself and following in her footsteps of drugs and stripping; her former abuser found her new phone number;

171 *Wishful Thinking: A Seeker's ABC's* (HarperOne, 1993), 118.

worsening carpal tunnel syndrome kept her out of work for the 24th week; and she was diagnosed with bipolar disorder.

All she could verbalize for the first five minutes was, "Abbie, I just wanna go home... I don't know where it is, or what it's about, but I know it's not here." Hope was on its last breath. It must be a grace that we don't experience being Homesick more often, or else I don't think we'd make it. I think we'd be willed about 33 years, tops, and that would be enough— that would be all our hearts could endure.

Most of our conversation was spent in despair, in unanswered questions of loss, death and confusion. But there were a handful on moments where my friend shared dreams for her shoe design, which "would forever change the fashion of walking." As she giggled about neon laces and the insignia on the sole, I knew she would make it through the night. Even if just for a few minutes, it was as if finding a space and language for her dream found a window to another world.

For we know that if the tent that is our earthly home is destroyed, we have a building from God, a house not made with hands, eternal in the heavens. For in this tent we groan, longing to put on our heavenly dwelling, if indeed by putting it on we may not be found naked. For while we are still in this tent, we groan, being burdened—not that we would be unclothed, but that we would be further clothed, so that what is mortal may be swallowed up by life. He who has prepared us for this very thing is God, who has given us the Spirit as a guarantee.

—II Corinthians 5:1–5

Teddy watched contentedly tonight as Elliana and I stacked blocks in the makeshift tent on the bottom bunk. We were safe and knew we belonged, the gray sheet framing our tiny reality and permitting us to soar beyond. God has long been privy to tents, in the wilderness and on the mountain, for protection and guidance, worship and rest, discernment and revealing glory. The Spirit, too, hovered like a safe tent at creation. Maybe heaven will have tents. *I need that safety, Father—that Kingdom sense over me this hour—the knowledge that you really are the Way, and that we're heading somewhere meaningful.*

Snuggling for some final minutes, I reminded Elliana that she's not to climb into Eden's crib.

"Do you understand, sweetheart?"

"Yes, Mommy, but you know I climb to Eden because I like him?"

"I do know that, and it's lovely that you like your brother. But you still mustn't climb into his crib tonight."

"Yes, Mommy. But maybe when I turn back to two, I'll be a baby again and can sleep with Eden in the crib."

"Yes, sweetheart, maybe."

Psychologically speaking, maybe pushing people toward their dreams is pulling them from reality. But realistically speaking, maybe reality is too much to bear at times, and yielding toward childhood—toward dreams and imagination—is the closest way home. "Truly, I say to you," Jesus said, "unless you turn and become like children, you will never enter the kingdom of heaven."[172]

---

172 Matthew 18:3.

Today has been a crappy day, Daddy, full of stupid plastic boats; even still, can you help me remember your benevolent, purposeful care? That trials with you mean weeping may tarry for the night, but joy comes in the morning? Please direct my sleep toward praise and belonging and the grace of tents.

Amen.

17. UNSTEADY

It may be on a kitchen floor,

Or in a busy shopping store,

Or teaching, nursing, day by day,

Till limb and brain almost give way;

Yet if, just there, by Jesus thou art found,

The place thou standest on is Holy Ground.

—M. Colley[173]

And then God answered: "Write this.

Write what you see.

Write it out in big block letters

so that it can be read on the run.

This vision-message is a witness

pointing to what's coming.

It aches for the coming—it can hardly wait!

And it doesn't lie.

If it seems slow in coming, wait.

It's on its way. It will come right on time.

—Habakkuk 2.2–3 (MSG)

---

173 R.J. Morgan. *Nelson's complete book of stories, illustrations, and quotes (electronic ed.)* (Nashville: Thomas Nelson Publishers), 796.

It feels like God should like me more today. Both littles were bathed, tickled, and fed. Laundry was washed (I don't iron), folded, and put away. I said something funny at Bible study and people laughed. I called two friends (versus typing to them). And Elliana asked the astute question en route to the Vietnamese restaurant: "Why don't we call him, Mr. God?" It was a good day. I'm in a good place. After months and months of not being there, it feels good. So good. Which gives me confidence to tell you about yesterday.

What if I cried out, "Daddy" as often as they cry out "Mommy?" my journal queried on what felt like the 1200th plea. It's been a less than mediocre mom day, and we just dropped off dinner to a ten-year-old neighbor recently diagnosed with cancer. Life feels exhausting and fragile and mean.

Micah was off work and we were ragged beyond repair. He sprayed all-purpose cleaner on a rag and wiped yogurt off Eden's face.

"Seriously?"

"What? It says 'all-purpose cleaner.'" (To this day he defends this case.)

"What about a movie," one of us suggested.

"Is that possible with them? Screen time is okay?"

"We'll make it possible. This is a moment of survival, not mature psychological and physiological discernment. Either we go psycho, or our children stare at a screen for a couple hours."

"Yes."

"Why don't you go pick up a pizza from Mellow Mushroom," he suggested. "The ride there might be nice." The 2.8 miles felt like a honeymoon with silence.

The four of us huddled on the couch with popcorn and a movie. Then we ate pizza. It was bliss. So far there are no signs of macular or brain degeneration. Frankly, the kids weren't even that interested, preferring stickers and mashing up pizza crust over the French film projected on the wall.

I wonder sometimes where our insanely hard and high expectations come from. We say and expect things of ourselves that we'd never in a million years put on another, lugging around the impossibly heavy burden of being perfect. When did holiness take on this qualification of perfection? One moment my primary pride is how you perceive me. The next it's how you perceive my children. If you perceive me, or them, as good, I feel good. If you perceive me, or them, as not good, I feel not good. Regardless though, all revolves around me. The pressure to be perfect and raise perfect kids and post perfect pictures is an uncontained and devouring wildfire in our mommy spheres.

The following verses stifle me: "On that day many will say to me, 'Lord, Lord, did we not prophesy in your name, and cast out demons in your name, and do many mighty works in your name?' And then will I declare to them, 'I never knew you; depart from me, you workers of lawlessness.'"[174] Sounds all too familiar. "God, I went to church, followed the rules, took Omega 3s, and prayed with the kids before bed." "Glad to hear it, Abbie, but were we friends today? Do you know me?"

It feels like we've stripped ourselves of permission to be weak (let alone

---

174 Matthew 7:22-23.

the fact that we've forgotten that weakness is a way to strength[175]). We've set a standard that moves beyond Jesus, reaching for the stars while he's contentedly settled right here where we are. We're saved by grace, it seems, and then start working again, as if Jesus' execution didn't *really* pay it all. As if salvation is about heaven, but the part between here and there still needs our tending to.

I used to sincerely wonder why Jesus went to the cross. It seemed a bit extreme. I was a decent gal—good, really—and quite liked the idea of being judged based on my rule-following. A gifted Pharisee has little fear of her external morale, it seems. What she fears is being seen inwardly—told at a heart level she's not guilty anymore; that she can rest; that she's saved by faith, not by works. The Pharisees were some of the smartest and most successful people of their day, and they missed God. Oh how that frightens my well-behaved persona.

> *No one can redeem the life of another*
>
> *or give to God a ransom for them—*
>
> *the ransom for a life is costly,*
>
> *no payment is ever enough.*
>
> *—Psalm 49:7–8 (NIV)*

Thank God my friend Chris told me during pregnancy, "The goal of the first five years is to help your kid stay alive." In other words, decisions about private or public or home or oils or dairy or diapering aren't gonna cause God to drop the sun. Much to my flesh's dismay, God isn't about performance and behavioral vows at the cost of forfeiting his unbreakable covenants of grace. He forgave me; now I'm invited to forgive myself. It's the side of God's character that's unscrupulously unjust—nonsensical in

---

175 See II Corinthians 12:10.

our comprehensions of reason—merciful points of common grace.[176]

Since being cast out of the Garden, it seems, our labor bears a restlessness and exhaustion we're unable to recover from, a fruit of thorns instead of grain.[177] We assign transcendence to things and people and duties that aren't meant to be transcendent.

I thought we did something special to cause Elliana's early and bountiful vocabulary—until a few weeks ago when our second child was found to have speech delays. Doing something special for Jesus apparently doesn't advance our successes. He's not looking for high-grade theology, or gold star morality. He's not wondering, "Did she raise a well-behaved, healthy, smart, likable, righteous, pretty, talented, ambitious, or socially acceptable enough kid?" Or, "Did she say, do, decide, pray, connect, awaken, play, or post enough as a mom?" "It is by grace you *and your children* have been saved, through faith—and this is not from yourselves *and your sacrifice to train them up with good behavior, or put them in private school, or pack them organic lunches, or cultivate their perfect well-roundedness...* it is the gift of God—not by works, so that no one can boast."[178] Success in the Christian life seems to boil down to an interaction when the end arrives—seeing our Savior face-to-face, stuttering through awestruck words, "I know you—you are he." To which he might graciously reply, "My darling child, I know you, too. Welcome home."

Jesus didn't have to do the baby thing, or the nailed to a cross thing. More pleasurable routes were available. But scars have always seemed to play a distinct role in the Christian story, and in the body of Christ. And he chose them. He chose to step from eternity, engaging skin and bones

---

176 "Common" because its benefits are offered without distinction, and it is "grace" because it is undeserved and completely orchestrated by God.
177 See Genesis 3:16–18.
178 Paraphrase of Ephesians 2:8–9; italics indicates added language.

and birth and death and time alongside a generation of first-century folks imaged after his Dad, *because he loves us.* He, too, came as a wanderer and a worker, laboring to death for our sake, bearing cosmic weights of homelessness and restlessness and exhaustion, allowing a crown of our thorns to be ground into his head. "He was pierced for our transgressions; he was crushed for our iniquities; upon him was the chastisement that brought us peace, and with his wounds we are healed."[179] Maybe scars don't make perfect sense of our stories, but they do seem to lend reminders. They remember, guarding our points of pain, documenting our trauma and displaying slivers of redemption. Scars mark my eternity, and they mark my today.

So easily I can find my work as a wife and a mom to grind me into the ground. As I attempt belief in the work of the cross, however, abiding *with* him in my labor, a transition seems to happen from fixation on the work to fixation on those served *through* my work. I am accepted and acceptable and enjoyable as Abbie today, not because dishes aren't crowding the counter (they are), or because my daughter didn't eat a roach yesterday (she did), or my son didn't flood a diaper in a ninety-five degree public place with no bathroom or spare (he did)—but because of the undeservedly bloody generosity of Jesus. Because of grace.

God doesn't like me more on days when my children are quiet in the checkout line, or when I have energy for sex, or when I separate laundry into personalized stacks. (Even as I write this these feel so pure and lovely and commendable.[180]) He doesn't like me less on days when my kid poops in the car seat, or I scream at the yellow light, or fantasize about toasting sayonara to the home life. He dwells *with me* in both extremes—and more profoundly, delights in me. *"Yes, Jesus loves me; yes, Jesus loves me; yes,*

---

179 Isaiah 53:5.
180 See Philippians 4:8.

Jesus loves me, the Bible tells me so."

For a while I carried around this note to myself: "The Sacrifice is finished. Stop striving, seeking an identity beyond you, spending yourself on a second crucifixion. Glory resides in you. Be still, beloved, and cast your cares upon him. Where you are weak, inadequate, boring, and insecure, he seeks you. Where you are ashamed, unlovable, disappointed, and tired, he loves you. Where you are addicted, adulterous, guilty, and greedy, he calls you his own. Where you are, he invites you." The note didn't heal me, but it did remind me I'm ever invited toward healing, toward believing we can only ever move toward God or away from him, and I want the former.

Dearest Trinity, would you hold me today, though my embrace isn't solid and my heart is unsteady? Please help me not to run ahead of grace today, the territory that tells me, "I can do it myself"—perfectly, even, in my distorted view—the territory that theoretically keeps everyone else happy, but slowly embitters and exhausts me. Please help me abide, knowing you are in the midst of me; I shall not be moved.[181]

---

181 Psalm 46.5a.

18. DUST

O guiding night!

O night more lovely than the dawn!

O night that has united

The Lover with His beloved

Transforming the beloved in her Lover.

—St. John of the Cross[182]

Blessed are those whose strength is in you, whose hearts

are set on a pilgrimage.

—Psalm 84:5 (NIV)

---

182 St. John of the Cross, *The Collected Works of St. John of the Cross*, trans. Kieran Kavanaugh and Otilio Rodriguez (Garden City, NY: Doubleday, 1964), 296.

The littles are keeping each other awake, exchanging their own version of farts and hilarious animal noises. "Mommy says you're her little slow poke, Eden," she reminded him a few minutes ago. It's true. He "stops and smells the roses," then befriends them for a meal, dessert, and siesta. Eden seems to grasp that life has ample worry and hurry of its own, and we mustn't add to the mix.

I rock on the porch, recollecting the day and how pummeled I've felt lately by the second most important commandment: "Thou shalt love thy neighbor as thyself."[183] I don't love my neighbor. I don't even like her.

The cicada's song is strong and united through the mossy trees above. It's sobering to imagine that over the next month it will fade into clusters of moaning as they slowly die off.

It's Ash Wednesday. Our 6 p.m. service reminded me that I am but dust; we are dust, God's beloved dust. I need to be editing the first draft of this book. Instead I start browsing adoption organizations and narratives—so much abandonment and neglect and abuse, so many corrupt systems. (America's isn't a bowl of cherries in this conversation either, mind you.) A year into marriage we "started trying" or stopped "not trying." Within months I was puking in the best of ways, and my pee caused two lines. Same thing happened for our second. At points in both pregnancies, I struggled to reconcile introducing new life to a broken world where millions were already desperate for a mommy and daddy. Pregnancy found me honored beyond measure, but also confused by orphans and sovereignty, frailty and our children's frailty.

"For you are dust, and to dust you shall return," Father Marc said, gently drawing the sign of the cross on Elliana's forehead.

---

183 Matthew 22:39b (KJV).

From a young age, I've known the shape of expectancy to be stunningly beautiful; I've also known a primal longing, or maybe calling, toward adoption. I was raised with decent awareness of global poverty, but living at an orphanage in my mid-twenties found me no longer analyzing a crisis from afar, but experiencing it. From that day forward, whether orphans or refugees, famine or disease, I wanted to be part of the fight. Fast forward a decade, when Micah tapped my shoulder at 2 a.m. some nights ago. "I'm ready, and it feels like God is saying we're ready. Our third child shall be through adoption."

We've since decided on India and dived into home studies and dossiers and waiting. We're waiting still. Apparently the wait for home is nearing its end. Apparently that's what the early church saints thought, too.[184]

....

It's upsetting to me sometimes why Jesus didn't completely heal everyone he came into contact with. Why he left earth with desperate and sincere longings left unfulfilled, bodies unhealed, prayers unanswered. Not unlike today, I suppose, when I wrestle with God not healing every deformity and calamity and disappointment.

A close friend and her husband reside in Uganda and have adopted five children orphaned by AIDS. Recently they had their first biological child, born with severe special needs. *Why, Lord? You know better than I how radically faithful is this hurting couple. Why did you do this to them? Shouldn't they get a break, let alone a reward? Why don't you simply heal her?* Another close friend, Jake, was a classmate in college. He took off a quarter to work at Waffle House, simply because he valued an eclectic livelihood and thought it would be enriching. Diagnosed with a brain tumor a year

---

184 See Revelation 3:10–11.

after we graduated, Jake asked God not to heal him, knowing he currently felt closer to home than ever, and should God heal him, he'd no doubt lose the matchless intimacy his tumor had brought about. I want to crave Christ like that.

Saints throughout history have grown frustrated by God, begging for blessing, altered timing, or circumstance. They stay thankful for about ten minutes, then grow frustrated again, cursing the Name that got them to gratitude in the first place. Even Jesus' most intimate followers got stuck in this mud. For three years a tribe of friends walked, talked, traveled, sang, fasted, and feasted with Jesus; they witnessed water being changed into wine, and multitudes being fed with five loaves and two fish. Yet when the day came for their supposed Messiah's murder, this unexpected turn was too much; they denied knowing him and went fishing. The magnificence of Jesus, apparently, is not for the doubtless and perfected, but for the hungry and the willing.

"Before I formed you in the womb I knew you,

and before you were born I consecrated you;

I appointed you a prophet to the nations."

Then I said, "Ah, Lord God! Behold, I do not know how to speak, for I am only a youth." But the Lord said to me,

"Do not say, 'I am only a youth';

for to all to whom I send you, you shall go,

and whatever I command you, you shall speak.

Do not be afraid of them,

for I am with you to deliver you,

declares the LORD."

Then the LORD put out his hand and touched my mouth. And the LORD said
to me,

"Behold, I have put my words in your mouth.

See, I have set you this day over nations and over kingdoms,

to pluck up and to break down,

to destroy and to overthrow,

to build and to plant."

—Jeremiah 1:4–10

Part of you still thinks I'm lying, or God's lying. Or that life on earth is a
big fat, stretch mark of a lie. You think it's an impossibility that you can
be no more precious to God than you are in this moment. You think you
must do, or be, or go, or say, to have his love or earn his favor—to know
rest and peace in your deep. That's okay—part of me still buys into these
lies too. God is fascinated by us, though, and won't let up. "Fear not, for
I have redeemed you; I have called you by name; you are mine."[185] "I will
not leave you as orphans; I will come to you."[186]

For we know that the whole creation groans and suffers the pains of
childbirth together until now. And not only this, but also we ourselves,
having the first fruits of the Spirit, even we ourselves groan within ourselves,
waiting eagerly for our adoption as sons, the redemption of our body. For
in hope we have been saved, but hope that is seen is not hope; for who
hopes for what he already sees? But if we hope for what we do not see, with

---

185 Isaiah 43:1b.
186 John 14:18.

perseverance we wait eagerly for it.

—*Romans 8:22–25 (NASB)*

We passed a tree on our afternoon walk, its braided roots exposed from shifting tides, as if to acknowledge layers of life that kneel beneath the surface. It felt like a sonogram from creation, assurance that when we cannot see literal growth beneath the skin, God is yet at work.

The hardest time for me lately has been Thursdays from 10:30 to 11:00 a.m. The library on Bull Street hosts Storytime, where a room of Savannah littles gather with one or both of their proud parents to read happy books and sing happy songs like "The Itsy Bitsy Spider." Moms are immovably enamored of their child's every clap; dads dote as their darlings awaken to magical worlds of song and story and "blasting off like a rocket ship."

I, too, marvel in the joy these 30 minutes bring to my children, but similarly steward a wave of tears blurring my sight. Such intimate and personalized outpourings of one-on-one attention (let alone from one's father or mother) aren't the typical Thursday morning agenda in an orphanage. Another adoptive mom recently traveled to India to bring home her daughter. The living situation they brought her from had 28 kids living and sleeping in one big room, with two books and three toys. And no enamored mommies locked onto a daughter's every move. No safe daddies beaming with pride at a son's glory-filled imagination.

When the wave starts to rise on Thursday mornings, I'm learning to pray for my daughter, though she feels palpably distant in these playful half-hour sessions. I'm learning to pray that someone, some Amma angel in her orphanage, will look her in the eyes and dote on her for a few minutes— that they'll hold her little hand and count aloud as they number her toes. I'm praying that someone will speak words of beauty—my baby's beauty—into her delicate, little ears. And that by God's grace, she'll still trust enough to listen.

In his final hours, Jesus prayed to his Father, "My prayer is not that you take them out of the world but that you protect them from the evil one."[187] *Protect them,* maybe he alludes to here, *from the lie that I am not enough— that I left too early, came too late, didn't come at all. Protect them from being blind to my holy markings—to nail marks that formed stretch marks, growth marks, marks of proof that I am here, at work, sculpting beyond what they can see.*

In some mysterious way, my earthly sorrows and suffering are said to be Jesus,'[188] my stretch marks his. Stretch marks, though, are never the cornerstone of the story.

> *They walked up a hill outside the city. Jesus carried the cross on his back. Jesus had never done anything wrong but they were going to kill him the way criminals were killed. They nailed Jesus to the cross. "Father, forgive them," Jesus gasped. "They don't understand what they're doing." "You say you've come to rescue us!" people shouted. "But you can't even rescue yourself!" But they were wrong. Jesus could have rescued himself. A legion of angels would have flown to his side if he'd called. "If you were really the son of God, you could just climb down off that cross!" they said. And of course they were right. Jesus could have just climbed down. Actually, he could have said a word and made it all stop. Like when he healed that little girl, stilled the storm and fed 5,000 people. But Jesus stayed. You see, they didn't*

---

187 John 17:15 (NIV).
188 See Romans 8:17.

understand. It wasn't the nails that kept Jesus there. It was love.[189]

....

Micah and I returned down the aisle to Coldplay's, "Til Kingdom Come." Yes, I had a slight crush on Chris Martin, but the lyrics also seemed a meaningful send-off. Hard though it was to fathom that exuberant October day, our marriage soundtrack would end when our lives on earth did.[190] Somehow we wanted to amplify that brevity to ourselves, and to our witnesses, as well as amplifying a Kingdom soundtrack able to play through our funerals—a story that will sing through eternity.

Charcoal colored ashes remind me again tonight of this soundtrack, of earth as "heaven's womb, heaven's nursery,"[191] bearing life and hope and invitations Homeward. They remind me that "Earth has no sorrow that heaven can't heal,"[192] as hymn writer Thomas More penned centuries ago. That I am dust, and to dust I shall return, earthy and alive, ever longing for roots, for the roadway back to the ground from which I came, the ground toward which I am going. They remind me that something about the shape of expectancy is beautiful.

As a flower cannot be pulled into bloom, Lord, so my soul cannot be. Your makings of love, your restorations of love in me—your image in me—are a grace. Thank you. Though unsteady at times, I am learning a posture of belonging, the delicate bloom of my design. Calmed and quieted, like a weaned child with its mother,[193] I am learning to believe. Amen.

189 Sally-Lloyd Jones, "The Sun Stops Shining," in *The Jesus Storybook Bible*, (HarperCollins/Zonderkidz, 2007), 304.
190 See Matthew 22:30.
191 An image from 20th century philosopher, Peter Kreeft: "What Difference Does Heaven Make?" Peter Kreeft, accessed June 9, 2017, http://www.peterkreeft.com/topics/heaven-difference.htm
192 Thomas Moore. "Come Ye Disconsolate," in *Irish Melodies and Sacred Songs* (New York: Oakley, Mason and co, 1869).
193 See Psalm 131:2.

Then I saw a new heaven and a new earth, for the first heaven and the first earth had passed away, and the sea was no more. And I saw the holy city, new Jerusalem, coming down out of heaven from God, prepared as a bride adorned for her husband. And I heard a loud voice from the throne saying, "Behold, the dwelling place of God is with man. He will dwell with them, and they will be his people, and God himself will be with them as their God. He will wipe away every tear from their eyes, and death shall be no more, neither shall there be mourning, nor crying, nor pain anymore, for the former things have passed away." And he who was seated on the throne said, "Behold, I am making all things new." Also he said, "Write this down, for these words are trustworthy and true."

— Revelation 21:1–5

Fingerprints from these beloveds appear throughout this work. Each of your lives has been a meaningful grace to mine; thank you:
Laura, Deonna, Salina, Liz, Sarah, Stephanie...Kim, Sandra, Megen, Alyssa, Amy, Lindsay...Melissa, Kaitlyn, Megan, Caroline, Natalie, Susanne, Sonya, Emily, Marc, Louise, Claudia, Lindsay, Jane...Sara, Antonette, Bess, Jen, Hannah, Jesse, Gracie, Ellie, Jenn...Mom, Dad & Court. Many thanks also to Jessica, Anna, David & Kalos Press, Talbot's Institute for Spiritual Formation, Eden Village, Christ Church Anglican & the gals of Renew, Wesley Gardens Retreat, Hope Academy, Foxy Loxy & Cutter's Point Coffee.

DISCUSSION
QUESTIONS

CHAPTER 1: CHOPPED

1. This chapter begins with a tension between feeling whole and feeling chopped. What are some "parts" of your identity that shape who you are? (For some, drawing this may feel more accessible than explaining it with words. Feel free!)

2. When you hear the word "femininity," is there a positive or a negative connotation? Is a particular person or memory associated with that impression?

3. What are some hopes and fears you're stewarding at the start of this book and season of your life?

Deeper yet...

"God cannot find you more precious than He does in this moment." How does this statement land on you? If you're able, return to this question multiple times this week. Notice how your answer fluctuates, maybe based on the time of day, or a given day of the week. Also note what doesn't fluctuate.

CHAPTER 2: WOMB

4. What words are you drawn toward in the poem at the start of this chapter?

5. For what are you waiting this season? How is that wait affecting you?

6. Does anything stand out to you from the Old Testament story of Jephthah's daughter in Judges 11?

Deeper yet...

Carve-out some space this week (maybe even daily) to read and meditate on Romans 8:18-38. Where do you find yourself gravitating? How might the Lord be speaking to you through these passages?

CHAPTER 3: ACHE

7. Who or what comes to mind when you think about Christmas? Maybe there's an obvious smell, or sensation in your body when you consider this season. Describe that.

8. Consider the following quote: "Home was what I hated. And yet somehow my deepest longing was hidden in my deepest hatred. 'The ache for home lives in all of us,' said Maya Angelou, 'the safe place where we can go as we are and not be questioned.' I have the guy now and magical lights beam through pine needles in our living room. But if I listen closely enough, the homeward longing still lingers." How do you relate to these sentences? What longings are cultivated in you when you consider "home"?

9. Describe a wilderness you've experienced. What did it feel like? How were you changed by it?

Deeper yet...

Choose one of the passages written-out at the end of this chapter. Explore ways to engage with it this week—maybe try painting what it looks like to you, writing it out on your palm, or singing it over yourself in the car or shower.

CHAPTER 4: FORM

10. What are your impressions of Mary, the mother of God? If you could have coffee with her this afternoon, what might you ask?

11. What external, "add-on commandments" do you see among Christians today, communicating that we require Jesus plus something (a political party, good behavior, certain clothing or music, participation with a certain cause, etc.) in order to be saved? In what ways do you battle legalism in your own heart?

12. Who have you envied lately?

Deeper yet...

Each night before bed this week, do a bit of self-examination using Psalm 35:3: God, please, "Say to my soul, "I am your salvation!" Ask Him what idols, lies, or legalisms have shackled you today, maybe subtly, or maybe aggressively, with a deceitful message of forgiveness and making you whole. "If I just had ____," idols like to promise, "all would be well." Then pray something like, Father, unshackle me from believing the liberty of your everlasting love and salvation can come from any other source or name.

CHAPTER 5: WORTH

13. How have food and body image played into your story (positively, abusively, as an addiction, etc.?)

14. Do any parts of your life today cause you to wonder, "Could God really take my diseased and dead parts and bridge them into something lovely?"

15. Consider the following quote: "Seems like we Jesus-followers seldom believe what God says about us. And not knowing we're his beloved means we'll fight to death to become someone else's." Whose love and liking having you been fighting for lately?

Deeper yet...

What messages do you want people to think about you? Do you see this spilling-out in any unhealthy ways—at home, work, in your marriage, parenting, friendships? Spend some time this week pondering God's view of you, alongside your craving for man's admirable view. Maybe Isaiah 43:4a could be a starting point: "Because you are precious in my eyes, and honored, and I love you."

CHAPTER 6: MARKED

16. Expectations are powerful. When in your life have you assumed a person or situation would be a certain way, and it wasn't? How did those expectations and that process affect you?

17. Does anyone come to your mind when you read Paul's words about, "the hidden person of the heart with the imperishable beauty of a gentle and quiet spirit, which in God's sight is very precious" (1 Peter 3:3-6)? What causes you to say so?

18. Have you been "permitting space for your own vulnerable conversations and explorations of your body and sexuality with God" lately? If so, what have you been learning?

Deeper yet...

Spend some time this week reading through the body related prayers in this chapter. Where do you find yourself hovering? What parts of you are still longing for the Lord's healing? Share about this process with a safe friend.

CHAPTER 6: MARKED

19. Expectations are powerful. When in your life have you assumed a person or situation would be a certain way, and it wasn't? How did those expectations and that process affect you?

20. Does anyone come to your mind when you read Paul's words about, "the hidden person of the heart with the imperishable beauty of a gentle and quiet spirit, which in God's sight is very precious" (1 Peter 3:3-6)? What causes you to say so?

21. Have you been "permitting space for your own vulnerable conversations and explorations of your body and sexuality with God" lately? If so, what have you been learning?

Deeper yet...

Spend some time this week reading through the body related prayers in this chapter. Where do you find yourself hovering? What parts of you are still longing for the Lord's healing? Share about this process with a safe friend.

CHAPTER 7: NEIGHBOR

22. What are your impressions of hospitality? Who or what may've influenced this?

23. Consider the neighborhood and neighbors with whom God has situated you this season. How do you see him at work?

24. When in your life have you been falsely accused? What was that like?

Deeper yet...

Spend some daily time this week praying for your neighbors. Ask Jesus to help you see them as he sees them, breaking through hostility and bitterness. Pray that he would bless them. Maybe write a card saying you're thinking of and praying for a particular neighbor, or take a walk around your streets, praying as you go for whatever the Lord brings about.

CHAPTER 8: LIE

25. As you consider the list of "gains" in lying (and feel free to add your own), do any of them stand out ?

26. Consider a time when God took you from feeling overwhelmed by sin and darkness, to feeling forgiven. Describe what this process was like.

27. Maybe there's something shameful, sinful, or scary that you've been wanting to tell someone, or tell God. (He already knows it, and loves you yet, but there's still something healthy and cathartic about acknowledging and exploring it with him). Spend some time this week pondering your inclinations to hide. Ask the Lord for courage to tell the truth, and to believe that it really is the truth, and only the truth, that sets us free.

Deeper yet...

Each day this week, find a comfortable place to sit, close your eyes, and for a handful of minutes, "let God look at you." Try to not to talk, but listen. Try not to defend, but receive. Try not to hide. In what ways is this practice uncomfortable? In what ways is it inviting? Notice how it may be different one day from the next. Share about this experience with someone you trust.

CHAPTER 9: REST

28. How does your heart feel toward God today?

29. What expectations do you feel God has on you? What expectations do you have on yourself?

30. If you are married, or with children, did marriage awaken any new emotions, or sides to yourself? How about parenting?

Deeper yet...

Practice the spiritual discipline of Sabbath this week. For a full day, cease from work and intentionally strive to enter God's rest, slowing down and choosing that which is life-giving. Share about (or participate in) this experience with someone else.

CHAPTER 10: MANNA

31. How has your relationship with God been affected by marriage (or by singleness)? How about by motherhood?

32. How have your experiences of marriage (or singleness) been different than what you expected? How about motherhood?

33. Is there something or someone you need to cheat on today, in order to prioritize abiding in God?

Deeper yet...

Take some time to envision your funeral. What do you want people to remember about you and the story you lived?

CHAPTER 11: AFTER

34. When in your life have you felt particularly fragile? Does any part of you feel fragile today?

35. What aspects of your life do you find meaningful?

36. If you're married, list five ways your husband and you "make love" apart from the physical act of sex. (There's no right or wrong here, and his answers may be different than yours. The exercise is about discovering ways you feel loved.) If you're single, list five ways you feel loved.

Deeper yet...

Take some time this week to write a letter to someone meaningful in your life.

CHAPTER 12: GROWTH

37. When is the last you remember feeling like you were a part of something that really mattered?

38. In what ways do you battle busyness?

39. What causes you to resist weakness, or being perceived as weak?

Deeper yet...

"In my experience, laying down, or doing something for God, isn't magic, but an invitation to commune with God. And over time, communing with God changes us. Or God changes us as we commune with him." What might you lay down for a day, or a week, or a season, in order to commune more deeply with God? As you explore this question with him, jot down what the conversation might look like if it were audible.

CHAPTER 13: BELONGING

40. "In some ways, the stay-at-home mom is just who I envisioned: satisfying, engaged, alive. In others, she's not. Her days are more busy and mundane than I envisioned, more simple and somehow chaotic, running

a jagged course I never knew possible, with meaningful highs and naked lows." If you're a mother, how do you relate to these words? (If you're not a mother, how has this season of your life been similar and different from what you envisioned?)

41. How does this chapter challenge your understandings of success and "being enough"?

42. "Maybe stretch marks have more to do with nail marks, and nail marks more to do with stretch marks, and love, than we account for? Maybe stretch marks prepare a way for resurrection? Maybe stretch marks are about Jesus, '...who for the joy that was set before him endured the cross, despising the shame, and is seated at the right hand of the throne of God.'" In what ways does your life today relate to this quote?

Deeper yet...

Further reflect this week on areas and relationships in your life where you struggle to feel like you're "enough." Where might these lies be coming from? What might God be inviting you to as you acknowledge and confront them? Share some of these thoughts with a safe friend.

CHAPTER 14: SAFE

43. When do you find belief in God to come most naturally? How about unbelief?

44. With whom do you feel safe? Share with someone three sentiments, or sentences, that you connected with in this chapter.

Deeper yet...

Multiple times this week, re-pose the following question in the context of your roles and current situation: How now shall I worship? Jot down your explorations and findings.

CHAPTER 15: NOISE

45. What stirs in you when you envision going on retreat, or getting alone with God?

46. If you're a mother, in what ways do you resonate with wanting to be the savior of your child's world? (If you're not, whose world are you tempted to try and control?)

47. How do you see God restoring areas of your life?

Deeper yet...

Prioritize an afternoon, or full day if you're able, just to be alone with God this week. Bring a Bible and journal and depending on the time of year, maybe head into the woods, or to a park, maybe to a museum, playground, or corner chair in a coffee shop. There is no goal on this date but to enjoy and be enjoyed by your Maker.

CHAPTER 16: TENT

48. What does it say about God that he has, "kept count of our tossings, that he has put our tears in his bottle"?

49. In what ways might your soul still be trying to catch-up with a transition in your life (moving, changing jobs, shift in a relationship, addition of a new child, etc.)? How might you allow some extra space for that process this week?

50. Recall some points in childhood where you felt safe and alive to dream. Do you feel this way now? If time, or money, or circumstances weren't a hindrance, what is one dream you have?

Deeper yet...

Become like a child this week and create a tent (or visit one already built in your midst). Crawl inside and spend some time playing and dreaming and pondering with God. Free yourself from expecting any massive revelations—they may come, but your agenda is simply being with the

Trinity and allowing him to be with you.

CHAPTER 17: UNSTEADY

51. When does it feel like God should like you more (theoretically)? What does this reveal about our understandings of grace?

52. How do you see pressures of perfectionism at work in your church family, friend group, and self?

53. Even as a follower of Jesus, saved by grace, how does earning God's favor and affections and forgiveness still entice you?

Deeper yet...

At the end of the chapter, Abbie talks about a note she carries around in her pocket. Find a sheet of paper and write out this note, maybe with her words, or maybe with your own, and likewise, carry it around for awhile.

CHAPTER 18: DUST

54. What does it mean to you today that, "you are dust, and to dust you shall return"?

55. What is one question you have for Jesus when you see him face to face?

56. Imagining yourself as a flower in bloom, what would you describe as your petals, and what are you asking of God today in their regard?

Deeper yet...

God graces our souls with stretch marks and uses them to further form us into the beauty of his image. Explore any stretch marks he may have surfaced in you throughout your reading of these pages.

ABOUT
KALOS PRESS

Kalos Press was established to give a voice to literary fiction, memoir, essays, poetry, devotional writing, and Christian reflection—works of excellent quality, outside of the mainstream Christian publishing industry.

We believe that good writing is beautiful in form and in function, and is capable of being an instrument of transformation. It is our hope and ambition that every title produced by Kalos Press will live up to this belief.

For more information about Kalos Press, *Stretch Marks*, and/or our other titles, or for ordering information, visit us on our website: www.kalospress.org

Or contact us by e-mail: info@kalospress.org

DIGITAL COPIES OF STRETCH MARKS I WASN'T EXPECTING

At Kalos Press, we've found that we often appreciate owning both print and digital editions of the books we read; perhaps you have found this as well. In our gratitude to you for purchasing a print version of this book, we are pleased to offer you free copies of the digital editions of *Stetch Marks I Wasn't Expecting*. To obtain one or more of these, simply visit the eStore of our parent ministry, Doulos Resources (estore.doulosresources.org) and enter the following discount code during checkout:

DiscountIWasn'tExpecting

If you purchased a digital edition, you may use the same discount code to receive a discount deducting the full price of your digital edition off of the purchase price for a print edition.

Thank you for your support!

CPSIA information can be obtained
at www.ICGtesting.com
Printed in the USA
FFOW03n0151030318
45404372-46100FF